A Practical Approach to Value Pricing

A proven pricing system for accounting and bookkeeping firms

By Mark Wickersham FCA

The most sought after profit improvement expert in the accounting community

ALSO BY MARK WICKERSHAM

Effective Pricing for Accountants

How to Build a Better Business and Make More Money: Simple Ideas That Really Work for Entrepreneurs

(with Steve Pipe)

How to Use Exhibitions and Conferences to Win More Business

(with Sarah Cross)

How to Build a Successful Bookkeeping Business

(with Jane Aylwin)

ISBN: 978-0-9928993-2-5

First published September 2016 by:
Mark Wickersham

Edited by:	Liz Morrell
Cover design by:	Noir
Typeset and page layout by:	Noir
Printed in Great Britain by:	SR Print Management

www.wickersham.co.uk
www.EffectivePricingForAccountants.com

Dedicated to my partner Sarah Cross
who has played a critical part in helping me get this book written and published.

And to my three wonderful daughters, Gabi, Tasha and Lara.

I love you all.

"As always Mark Wickersham cuts to the heart of the matter. In his latest book: *A Practical Approach to Value Pricing* – Mark gives an abundance of practical tips and methods for any accountant to employ in their search to be 'something different' from the norm. The step-by-step approach Mark explains is not theory but taken from the real world where each of his ideas have been tested to produce the results he promises. If you're an accountant looking to deal with the challenges of a competitive world where audit work is increasing done by computer then Mark's latest book not only is a must for your bookshelf – it should be on the top of your reading pile too."

– Peter Thomson

"The UK's Most Prolific Information Product Creator"

"The accounting profession is changing and Mark is on the forefront of the revolution from billing by the hour to billing for the value provided."

– John Warrillow

Founder, The Value Builder System™
Author of "The Automatic Customer: Creating a Subscription Business In Any Industry"
& "Built to Sell: Creating a Business That Can Thrive Without You"

"Imagine running an accounting practice, where you are compensated in direct correlation to the tremendous value you bring to your clients. Imagine no more! Wickersham's newest book walks you step by step to running a very profitable accounting practice. If you are serious about moving your practice into the future, this is a must read book!"

– Mike Michalowicz

Author of Profit First and Co-Founder of Profit First Professionals

"By blending inspiring stories with detailed guidance, this brilliant book provides accountants everywhere with a blueprint for pricing success."

– Steve Pipe FCA

Author of "The world's most inspiring accountants"

"*Awesome*. From the moment you open this book you get that it's a *great* book from a great, unassuming guy. Mark's impact on the accounting profession is already *huge*. This book takes it massively higher. It's a book to get, to read, to act on and to cherish. It changes lives... maybe even yours."

– Paul Dunn

Regarded by many as the 'Godfather of Business Development' for Accounting firms and now co-founder and Chairman of B1G1: Business for Good.

"I completely agree that value pricing is a critical skill for accountants to become capable of. It's like learning to write left-handed after using your right hand for so long – you understand the theory but practice is needed. Mark's book is brilliant at helping accountants learn the skills to implement value pricing successful. Essential for all fee earners!"

– Gordon Gilchrist

Co-founder & Marketing Director 2020 Group

"*A Practical Approach to Value Pricing* is quite simply a must-read for all independent bookkeepers and accountants. Due to the major disruption now going on in the accounting world with automation, outdated hourly pricing methods will literally put us out of business! But this treasure of a book shines a light on the path to successfully navigate the journey to value pricing, well past the fuzzy concepts we've been hearing for years. It focuses on the actual steps to make the switch, which are brought to life by the many real world experiences of accountants and bookkeepers who have embraced Mark Wickersham's methods. Even when executed only partially, these firms are seeing amazing results, and quickly! This is the ultimate guide to short-cutting the transition to value pricing. Highly recommended."

– Gabrielle Fontaine

Author of The Freelance Bookkeeper Blog

"My kind of book. Clear, succinct, practical, tells you the 'how to...' and is full of real case studies and examples."

– Robert Craven

Author, Grow Your Service Firm

Contents

FREE RESOURCES AND SUPPORT

Thank you so much for ordering my book. It means so much to me.

And if you enjoy it, please REVIEW this book on Amazon. I need your feedback to make the next version better. Thank you so much.

And to thank you I have some free resources and support for you.

Free book
If you have not yet read my first book, "Effective Pricing for Accountants" you can read 3 of the chapters for free. Those chapters are contained within my eBook, "How to Price Accountancy Services for Maximum Profit" you can grab a copy here:

www.EffectivePricingForAccountants.com

Free training
If you want to make the transition to value pricing I have created a training programme to teach the foundations and I'm happy to let you have a copy for free. You can register your copy here:

markwickersham.mykajabi.com/store/AWdTeT6J

Free advice and support
I regularly post videos on my YouTube page. Subscribe to it here:

www.youtube.com/user/Pricing4Accountants

When you Like my Facebook page you will get notified of new content and blog posts. You'll find it here:

www.facebook.com/markwickershamfca

And connect with me on LinkedIn here:

www.linkedin.com/today/author/markwickersham1

FOREWORD

We live in exciting times

"Use a pricing system. It gives you so much confidence when you can sit down with a client or a prospect and go through each individual item, explain to them what's involved and talk them through the price. It makes pricing at the level that we should be pricing so much easier."

— Jane Aylwin, APB Associates

There are some big changes happening in the accounting profession, which create a huge opportunity for accountants and bookkeepers that want to grasp it and make a huge difference to their clients' lives. To do that though, we have to also make sure that we change our pricing models.

Back in May 2011, my first book was published. "*Effective Pricing for Accountants*" hit the number one spot on Amazon across all business books within a week of publication. This was against more than a million business books, beating titles such as *"What you see is what you get"* by Alan Sugar and *"Who Moved My Cheese"* by Dr Spencer Johnson.

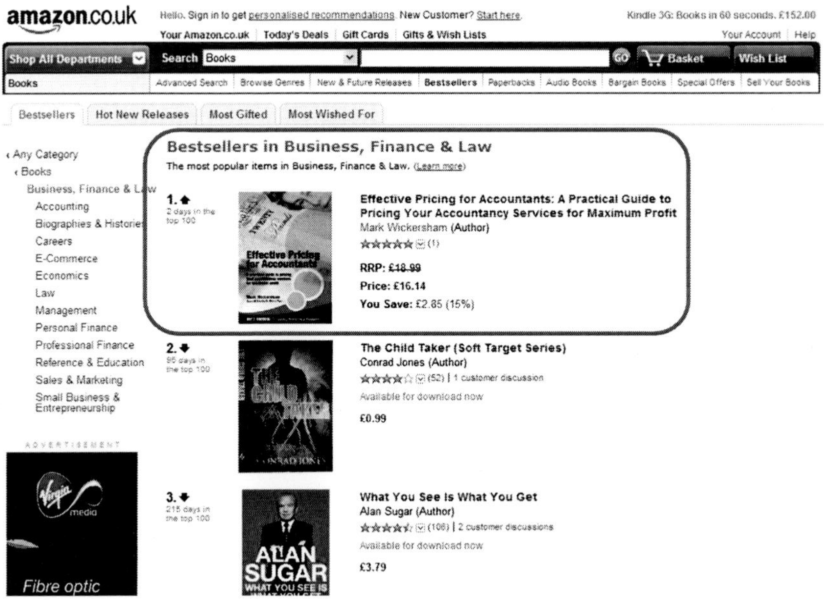

Since then, as a result of writing that book, I have had the pleasure and honour to speak and share my message in many countries around the world. I have been across to Australia to speak, to the U.S. and I have just come back, at the time of writing this book, from the Bahamas. I will be speaking in Canada very soon, and of course I also regularly speak throughout the UK.

I have had the pleasure of meeting some extraordinary accountants and bookkeepers who have been brave enough to grasp this new opportunity and are doing things differently and getting better results.

Why this book is a practical approach

This book is going to be picking up on where *"Effective Pricing For Accountants"* left off. If you have not read that book then I strongly recommend you grab a copy.

In the opening to *"Effective Pricing for Accountants"* I shared my story. In case you've still to read it, very briefly I was in practice after starting my own accounting firm way back in 1996.

Within two and a half years I had grown very quickly but my practice was a mess. I had made so many crazy mistakes – the biggest of which was I had no idea how to price my services. In fact that was the case right up until 1999 when I came across one of my inspirations, Ron Baker.

I read Ron's book, *"The Professional's Guide to Value Pricing"* and a light bulb went on in my head. I figured out a different way, a better way to price. I created systems in my accounting firm that changed my results pretty much overnight. Certainly within six months I was getting much better prices and, as a result, significantly higher profits.

That enabled me a few years later to sell my accounting firm in a management buy-out. The firm still exists today.

I'm very privileged to have been able to teach accountants and bookkeepers ever since 2000 how to value price and, in particular, teaching a structure, a system, a framework they can use.

I've found that accounting and bookkeeping firms find moving to value pricing difficult. I think it is now widely accepted amongst the accounting profession that time-based billing has got to go and that we have to switch to value pricing. But increasingly firms are saying to me *"This is so hard, we don't know how to do it"*.

It's not surprising.

Firstly, value is very subjective. It's very difficult, if not impossible, to put any sort of quantification on value. Secondly, to make it even worse everybody values things differently. So when you are trying to value price your tax return service, for example, you are faced with the problem that every single client you talk to places a different value on you doing their tax return.

That is why value pricing is hard.

Back in the book *"Effective Pricing for Accountants"*, I talked a lot about some of the key issues with pricing, some of the key techniques and strategies that you should be using. What I want to do in this book is pick up where I left off previously.

A book in three parts

I have three objectives:

1. At the start of this book I will set the scene and explain why you need to change your pricing model fast. I'll introduce the problems with current pricing practice and the myths surrounding it.

2. I want to make it highly practical. I will share with you a framework to help you with implementing value pricing. A 7-step formula so you price the best way, consistently, with confidence.

3. I want to make it inspiring. Throughout the book the chapters will be supported by some of the many stories I have heard over the last few years from incredible accountants and bookkeepers.

About the inspiring stories

Since the last book was published in May 2011, I have heard so many great stories of firms that I have worked with that are getting incredible results. These stories are inspirational.

I mentor firms in the UK, Europe, the U.S., Canada and New Zealand. It is so rewarding working with so many great accountants and bookkeepers all around the world, and it is some of their stories that I am going to share with you in this new book.

The stories are based on interviews carried out by Sarah Cross over the last 12 months. Each story starts by telling you a little bit about the person. You can then read about their challenges, what they did to overcome them and the results they got. Each story ends with a handful of top tips from these accounting professionals.

Reading these tips alone is priceless. There is so much to be learned from accountants and bookkeepers that are leading the way in the value pricing revolution.

At this point I want to thank the firms who so kindly shared their stories and results.

To get us started I want to share two amazing stories that really set the scene.

The first one is from an accountant I have worked with for a number of years now. Michael Young is a forward-thinking accountant from New Zealand. The story that follows is in his own words (completely unedited); and it's inspiring.

In particular, what I want to draw your attention to is the end of the story, where Michael lists in bullet point form some of his key insights and learnings around pricing. Make sure you check these out because each of the key insights that Michael has referred to I will be picking up on and explaining in more depth later on in the book.

The second story that I want to share with you in this introduction is an extraordinary UK bookkeeper called Jane Aylwin. She sent me the story that follows a little while ago when she was getting some early successes. It's inspiring in itself, but actually what's interesting is that since she wrote it her story has got bigger and better still.

I have been working very closely with Jane and so, at the end of this book I will reveal the second part of her story so you can see just how far she has come.

I hope you enjoy reading this book, and most importantly I hope you take some action. And when you get great results please, please tell me all about your successes. You never know, you might appear in the next edition of this book.

Mark Wickersham FCA
The most sought after profit improvement expert in the accounting community

www.wickersham.co.uk

“

I was able to improve fees by 200%

Michael Young, Young & Associates, New Zealand (In his own words)

Background
I started my sole practice in the year 2000 in Wellington, New Zealand.

Pricing Challenges
Like Mark, in his earlier practice, I discounted fees to attract clients on price on what was largely tax compliance work. This led to declining profit margins, so to maintain my net income I had to do more work. It became a numbers game, working harder for less – it was like being on a treadmill.

Clients would leave when the next tax year came around if they found another accountant offering a lower price, so I was competing on price and not on service. The work became less rewarding and therefore less enjoyable.

Achieving Success
To gain better financial success I sought different clients in the hope that some would pay higher prices. But it was not easy as the work remained largely compliance in nature, i.e. clients paid

for the work because it had to be done rather than their wanting it to be done. I could not raise the perception of value. I took every opportunity to raise prices but the opportunities to do this were few and far between. I then progressed to diversifying services then service bundling – this achieved modest success.

The turning point

It was purely by chance that I came across Mark Wickersham's email address at the bottom of someone else's email so I clicked it and this lead me to some of Mark's videos on YouTube. I followed through and came across Mark's video promoting his online course on value pricing. It was a good offering so I took up the middle option.

That was in May 2014 and I have never looked back!

Mark's guidance and logic was so good I couldn't fault it as a qualified Chartered Accountant with significant practical experience in family businesses. Like some of Mark's course subscribers, I became enthused by the material and completed the one-year course in three months. I took lots of notes as Mark recommended and this helped me understand the concepts behind the material.

Success at last!

In May 2015 a lead I initiated earlier brought a new client to us. This client operated three businesses. The ownership of the businesses was about to change and the client was looking for new accountants. We were in the right place at the right time.

Having learnt Mark's value pricing methods I prepared a service needs analysis for this client followed by a proposal offering the 3, 4 and 5 star packages with top-down pricing. The client signed up for the 4-star package, but said they really wanted 5-star but needed to improve the businesses to make it affordable.

The value pricing principles and methods Mark taught me definitely work and they offer great opportunities for both cross-selling and up-selling. By cross-selling through the packages I was able to ***improve fees 200%*** on what we would otherwise have.

Furthermore, this same client recently established another business and it was easy to offer him the same packages for the new business. He opted for the 4-star package again as a starting point. This amounts to an additional $15,000 straight to the bottom line from cross-selling alone and we still have the opportunity to up-sell. The client is very happy with the service packages for his multiple businesses and perceives excellent value and a sense of progress.

We also benefit from and enjoy new professional work, which is progressing towards value-added services. The client is mindful of the fact that the 5-star package is available and offers much more services that will improve his businesses and personal well-being. We are working to achieve this.

Onward and upward

We are now introducing our value pricing packages to existing clients through the Cloud Pricing software and it is being well received. Cloud Pricing offers new opportunities for us to also sell our specialist services and also offers a new experience for clients to appreciate what additional services are available to them – they love the opportunity to cherry-pick services beyond compliance services.

We will progress to new clients as we approach the new business and financial year commencing this April. We can now look forward to more enjoyable and profitable professional work and attracting better quality clients. It helps to identify and weed out the poor quality clients. We feel we are now being valued as true professional advisors and not just glorified number crunchers. It's absolutely win-win and enlightening.

The key learning points:

- Value price and don't price on time
- Offer upfront fixed prices to give clients price certainty – no surprise bills
- Explain the value of services offered
- Link the value to the price
- Offer a suite of services that gives clients choice that meets their needs
- Only offer services you have competence to offer so you don't under-deliver – build your competency areas
- Maintain close professional relationship with clients – be visible, be contactable and be connected
- Offer the occasional freebie
- Express appreciation that they are valued clients

A bookkeeper now puts real value on her work

APB Associates was founded in 2009 by Jane Aylwin and is now based in Pulborough, West Sussex. Jane worked by herself until 2013 when she took on her first employee. She now has two full time and two part time team members.

Unusually for the case studies in this book, APB Associates is a bookkeeping firm rather than an accountancy practice. And that was one of the issues for owner Jane Aylwin.

"Although we provide quite a lot of accountancy support in terms of management accounts, cashflows and reporting, we are predominantly bookkeeping and I was finding it very, very difficult to communicate the value of actual bookkeeping. People don't see it as a high value service," Jane says.

The result of this was an inconsistent approach to pricing her services. "It was very much what day is it, which way is the wind blowing, what does it look like the client can afford? There was absolutely no structure to it at all and I found pricing so, so difficult. I always based it more on what I thought the client would pay than what was the right price for what they wanted."

What made all the difference to Jane was finding a pricing system that systemised the process. And the success of that has helped to change her attitude too, so before setting a price she now considers what the job is worth both to the client and to herself.

A test she carried out on a group of tax return clients has reinforced the value of the new process.

"Historically they have hardly paid anything at all. They've always brought their paperwork in on 28 January and it's always been a nightmare as it's a plastic bin liner full of screwed up bits of receipts. What's more, they were all very bad payers too so I'd do their tax return within the time frame of two days that they gave me and it would take them six months to pay. Which really is hardly fair! And I thought, is it actually worth keeping that money under those terms? And the answer was 'no'. So I'll go back to them and I'll more than double the fee, give them a deadline and ask them to pay upfront. If they say 'no' I really haven't lost anything."

Jane identified six of the worst offenders and emailed them to explain that she wouldn't be able to complete their tax returns unless the paperwork was sent in by 31 October. "Three of them found somebody else to do it cheaply and at the last minute (which is absolutely fine), but with the three that remain we're actually earning more than we were with the original six. They brought their stuff in on time and they paid upfront, which is something I would never have dared to ask for before."

And when a potential new client needed help with forecasts for a business plan that meant Jane working over a Bank Holiday, she made sure she charged a worthwhile price. "I thought what am I prepared to give up my Bank Holiday Monday for, what's that actually worth?"

Jane's solution was to offer the client three options – forecasts for one year, two years or three years. "Previously I would have done a five year forecast for £500 and worked all the Bank Holiday and not even thought about it. Because the attitude was, I must get a potential new client, even for just £250. This time, all the options I gave her were three times what I would have charged previously, but she went for the middle option and paid straight away."

Jane now has an ambitious plan to increase her average fees by around 230% over the next two years. "We'll definitely be changing our client base, but we aren't looking at getting a higher volume of clients. I think it's doable using the new pricing tools and with our new confidence. We're right at the beginning of the journey, but I'm pretty positive that it's going to be possible."

The key learning points:

- Use a pricing system. It gives you so much confidence when you can sit down with a client or a prospect and go through each individual item, explain to them what's involved and talk them through the price. It makes pricing at the level that we should be pricing so much easier.

CHAPTER ONE

The problem with being cheap

Before we get to the all-important formula I mentioned, we need to set the scene and to explain why change is needed.

Over the next few chapters I will do that, explaining about the problems of being cheap; some of the myths around pricing; sharing the biggest mistakes we make and explaining the big opportunity facing the accounting profession. I will also give you some thoughts on why it is good to be small.

Once I've done that you can find out more about the framework in Chapter 7.

One of the things I constantly witness is almost the entire accounting and bookkeeping profession is too cheap. When I speak to accountants and bookkeepers at events I always ask whether they feel they are working too many hours, too hard and for too little reward.

Guess what? Everybody's hands go up.

The reason for that is because as an industry we are not charging enough. We have to put our prices up, but there are often a couple of reasons holding us back from doing so.

The first of those is confidence. We don't fully appreciate the difference that we can make to people's lives and the value that we have to offer – something I believe bookkeepers are even more guilty of than accountants. Many bookkeepers think, *"It's just bookkeeping"*.

The three compromises we make

We're too cheap. And, believe it or not that causes most of our problems. In fact my good friend, Steve Pipe (author of *"The world's most inspiring accountants"*), talks about the three compromises we make when our prices are too low.

Firstly, it means that our income is too low and, as a result we sacrifice both our profits and our income when we are too cheap.

Because of that we end up compromising our work-life balance. In other words, we work harder to try to make up for our reduced income and profits and overstep a healthy balance.

The third compromise that we make, whether we mean to or not, is we cut corners. We often miss out on opportunities to add more value to the client because we are so busy trying to get the compliance work done, getting the data processing done, doing the accounts, doing the bookkeeping.

So why are we too cheap?

The big issue holding us back

I mentioned earlier that confidence is a big issue; in fact I would say confidence is the number one thing you have to get right when it comes to pricing. If you are not confident with the way you price you will never get the right price. Instead you will focus on being competitive to try and win the work. Yet when you become confident you will get better results.

So how do you gain that much needed confidence?

Confidence comes from two things; firstly confidence comes with having the knowledge; the understanding; the training on how to value price; and secondly confidence comes from having a structure, a system, a framework.

We're going to look at both of those issues throughout the rest of this book, and you will probably notice in many of the success stories the word 'confidence' surfaces repeatedly. So often I find that firms who are getting great results say to me: *"I now have the confidence"*.

Confidence is about a mindset. You have probably at some point had a client say to you, *"That's a bit more expensive than I was expecting"* and, as a result, you assume that client is price sensitive. In fact, not only that, but when you have heard that comment two or three times, you then tend to make the assumption that all your clients are price sensitive. I will come back to that later on.

Why you want to hear that intake of breath

However, here is the key point. If you never get anybody say to you, *"That's more than I was expecting, that's a bit expensive"*, then it is telling you you're too cheap. Although you may hate it when people say, *"That's expensive"* you should welcome it. You need to learn to recognise that when clients say that to you it means you're starting to push the boundaries with your pricing, you're starting to get the right prices. If nobody says it to you, you're too cheap.

So the key learning point for this chapter is you absolutely must start pushing your prices up because I can pretty much guarantee that you are too cheap. Not only is it the right thing to do for you – it means that it will help with your income, you'll start working less hours and you'll get your work-life balance back – but it's also the right thing for the client.

Now that might sound counter intuitive, but remember the three compromises from earlier? What I have seen time and time again within the profession is that because we're too cheap we end up doing the bare minimum that we need to do to get the job done, and yet as a profession we have the ability to change people's lives.

That life-changing moment can come through tax planning and reducing tax bills, or helping them to increase the profits of their business by increasing margins or helping to reduce their cash problems through helping them collect money. Whatever it is we can change people's lives. When we put our prices up it gives us the space, it gives us the budget, and it gives us the time to enable us to spend more time with those clients figuring out other ways that we can add more value.

Inspiring stories

What follows are the stories of four accountants that I want you to read. These four are all sole practitioners talking about how they put up their prices, and the results they got from doing so. You will see some interesting themes start to emerge.

The classic mistake new start-ups make all the time

Andrew Hardy has been running his practice in Frome, Somerset, for the last 18 years. He and his wife are the only full time employees and they use two sub-contractors when needed. Turnover is around £80,000 per year.

Andrew Hardy's biggest problem when he started his practice was that he had no clients. Not one. So his very justifiable fear of not earning enough income led to him making a classic mistake.

"I went in cheap," he says now. "My overheads were low so I knew I could afford to compete on price. And it worked; I got quite a few clients in a short space of time."

What Andrew didn't realise at the time, of course, was that he was creating big problems for himself further down the line.

"Turnover in the first 10 years was never more than about £25,000-£30,000, which was OK to live on," he explains. "In fact I was doing better than when I was employed, by the time the tax advantages were taken into account. But it wasn't anywhere near my market rate or the potential of the practice."

And Andrew found that his clients expected a lot for their money. "Going in too cheap tends to attract cheap clients and often they expect you to do an awful a lot for their 25p (which in fact was what I charged one client because that's all he had!). And I found I was pricing in such a way that I was getting a lot of business and spending a lot of time on it, but not making a lot of profit."

Andrew had cautiously started to put up his prices before he started working with Mark. There had been no resistance at all to the increases so he suspected that he should go further; exposure to Mark's ideas confirmed this. So he began to increase his prices more aggressively.

Mark had warned him that he might lose one or two clients, though the gains would more than compensate for that. But in fact, Andrew didn't lose any at all. "We gained clients. It was the old story – if you are too cheap, people believe you can't do it for that money. So it actually improved our credibility. And a couple of times people said they were glad I had come to my senses and was charging a realistic price." Andrew now increases his prices every year.

Another element of his pricing strategy was to review the clients for whom he had historically done a lot of work for a small fee. "I simply put up the prices and said to people, "You know, you have had this discount for years. I am not going to do it anymore. I can't afford to." And again we haven't lost any clients, but we have been able to get a more reasonable rate for the job."

He has also become quite strict about pricing work for new clients. "When we have new work or something special, I tend to price that high for two reasons. One, the client needs the service quickly and two, because new and special work disrupts the orderly routine of the practice. We've got to stop doing other things and we should be compensated for that. It can mean delaying regular clients' stuff and I am not prepared to do that without getting paid for it."

The impact on Andrew's profits has been significant. "It's had a very good effect; probably £20,000-£30,000 more in profit. Obviously price increases don't involve extra costs so that's been nice."

And perhaps more importantly he now sees his practice in a different light: "It's also made me look more critically at the business as a business rather than as a practice. So my wife and I are continually asking, 'Why are we doing this? And what should we be doing in this practice?'"

The key learning points:

- Find a support group like Mark's. As well as the handholding from Mark, the other benefit is the interchange between the various participants. People who have the same problem as you and have a solution will share that with you, and all you've got to do in return is reciprocate.

- If you can't join a group, do what I did. Review your prices, look at the market around you, and look at your service delivery. Our levels of service delivery have improved because if you do put up prices you feel you should give something more, and we do. We almost always do a quick review of profitability and suggest at least one financial strategy going forward and people really value that.

The right pricing strategy creates the right work-life balance

Lenah Oduor is a sole practitioner in Banbury, Oxfordshire. She set up her practice, gHawk Accounting, in 2013 after being made redundant from her previous job with the County Council. She runs the practice on a part-time basis to fit in with caring for her young children.

Having previously worked only in business or in the public sector, when Lenah Oduor started her practice she came up against a big challenge straight away. How much to charge?

"I was only used to working on one section of the finances, but now I would be providing small business owners with an all round service. And I didn't really know how to price it. I always bundled the accounts and tax returns together, but then I wouldn't charge for the bookkeeping. So my biggest problem was knowing what to charge first of all and how to put a value on the other things I was doing."

Lenah started working with Mark in 2014 and gradually began to try out some of the ideas he introduced her to. To find out what prices clients would actually pay, she tested menu pricing, offering three different packages for every service she offered.

"I sat down and practiced, then had more meetings and tested the reaction. I amended my pricing to make sure that I was charging for everything, so the first time I did, it I left certain things out. Then I kept adding more in to make sure that my client's needs were being covered in at least one of the three packages."

She also started to use direct debits (via GoCardless) with her clients, which had an immediate impact on cashflow both for them and for her. "I didn't have to wait too long to get paid because I made sure there was a plan in place to be paid by the time the work was completed," she says.

More success came with using brochures that explained step-by-step the work she was doing. "I did a quote a few months ago for somebody who runs a recruitment company," Lenah explains. "They had twenty members of staff who were seasonal, working different hours. I took him through the services that I could offer, step-by-step using the brochure, and he actually said to me that his previous providers were not giving him a proper explanation about the value he was getting for the money he was putting in. And that by looking through the brochure I had made him aware of certain things that he wasn't perhaps considering for his staff. It almost ended up that I had made him aware of his other responsibilities as an employer. He was very grateful for that and was able to work with a HR person to sort it out."

As a result of these new ways of working, Lenah has now replaced her old salary while still working part-time, something she never thought she would be able to do. "My fees have definitely gone up, which means I can work with fewer clients and deliver a better quality service instead of chasing a lot of £100 tax returns which is perhaps what I did in my first year."

More than anything though, Lenah now has confidence that she is delivering a service that is valuable to her clients. And the confidence to charge prices that reflect that value.

"I don't feel under pressure when I go into meetings with prospects or clients because I know I'm laying out a structured way of working and they can choose at what level they want to work with me. I am accountable on an item-by-item basis in terms of what I deliver to the client. They know what they are getting and I know what I'm delivering. It just makes the work so much easier to deliver."

The key learning points:

- Understand the value that you bring to the client. It takes a long time to get an accountancy qualification and there is great value in that, which we are perhaps sometimes blind to. Our customers don't always know the value we can bring so we owe them a duty to explain to them exactly what we do, step-by-step.
- Never have one price. Always give the customer a choice so that the customer is actually doing the pricing themselves. Give them a choice, show them what you can offer and let them decide where they want to come in. Then they feel they are in control of the situation and not that you are doing things for them. It creates a relationship so you can negotiate things going along and keep in touch on an on-going regular basis.

"I realised that if I wanted to look after my clients properly, I had to increase my fees."

Wagner CA is a small general practice with a team of 6 and offices in Glasgow, Edinburgh and London. The practice started in 2002 and currently has a turnover of around £300,000.

With a practice that has grown every year since it started – even through the recession – Leo Wagner is obviously doing something right. And his discovery of what was the right thing to do came a few years after he started his practice.

"About ten years ago I spoke to an accountant who wanted to sell me his fees," Leo explains. "I asked him when was the last time he'd increased his prices and he said, 20 years ago. And I thought to myself, that's why you've got health problems and that's why you can't service your clients. It was a bit of an 'Aha' moment. So I thought to myself, I need to put my prices up to look after my clients. Doing that forces you to do a fantastic job because you're charging them more than average so they expect more. It forces you to be fantastic at what you do – and that's not a bad thing."

Leo has found the best way to test his prices is to increase them regularly to find the 'bite point'. His price for a year-end set of books used to be £850 but a few years ago he increased that to £1050. Within a year he had increased it again to £1250. "Now, there aren't that many clients who I charge £1250 plus VAT for a set of financials because it's all wrapped up in the price," Leo says. "But that's the benchmark. Instead of £850 being the benchmark, within two years it had gone up to £1250 and I recognised that that's the bite point. Mark often talks about putting your prices up until you start to see some sort of feedback. So it's been very useful to have that benchmark."

And he's confident that he's doing the right thing. "I don't want to race to the bottom with pricing so if someone starts trying to negotiate with me about going elsewhere I just say, 'look it sounds like this guy is doing you a very good deal on the price' and I let the prospect go away. That happened with one prospect who was the wife of an existing client, a very good client. She's a lawyer and she got an alternative quote and went with them. Within six months she was back and said, 'I'll pay you what you want.' It's often just about having the courage and confidence to adjust your prices."

The feedback Leo gets from his clients is good, and they put the emphasis on the service they get from him, not the cost. "Profits are going up and up," he says. "Turnover is roughly £300,000 plus VAT and profit is above £200,000 so it's a very small practice but a very profitable one. But that's not to say that there isn't still a lot of work to do. And the one thing I learn constantly is that you constantly learn. The more you learn the more you realize how much more you have to learn and that's so true of me. I've stumbled my way through to that kind of profit level and I've still got lots to do. I'll keep learning until I take my last breath."

The key learning points:

- Don't let price be the defining factor when you meet a prospect. Make it the quality and range of your services. You can refer them on for more specialised services even if you don't provide them yourself.

A change in attitude made all the difference to this small practice

Tina Jenkins is based in Llantwit Fardre, South Wales, and runs her practice with the help of a part-time PA. Although she started her practice in 2012, she only began to work on it full time in 2015 and she now has around 12 clients.

As someone who regularly advised her clients not to give advice away for free, Tina Jenkins found that all too often she was doing exactly that – giving advice or even doing work without charging for it.

"One thing I don't like doing is talking to people about money. I work mainly with lawyers and I'm forever telling them how to maximize their profits. But when it comes to me it's a different story! I've always shied away from discussing money to the point that, if somebody asked me how much I charged, I've not even wanted to go back to them with a price. I always felt as though I had to do things free or cheap – so I probably have lost work because of it," she explains.

But Tina has now started to change the way she runs her business and it's already making a big difference.

"Now, I really think about the service I'm offering and I chunk it down," she says. "So I'll say a forecast is £X, your annual accounts would be £Y and so on. Recently someone came to me via the website for a company accounts job. She's a very small business and I quoted £300 to do the job. Then when I met her again it came to light that actually she needed self-assessment doing so I said I'd charge her for that. Then it came to light that actually it wasn't just this year's self-assessment, she hadn't filed for last year either. And then she came back to me with a fine of £150 because she hadn't filed. And instead of just saying, look I'll do it for you, which I have done in the past, I actually charged her for doing it. And then she didn't give me the right information so the return went off and I had to amend it! I was adamant that I wasn't going to do it for free which I would have done previously so I went back to her and I charged her again and she was more than happy to pay me.

"And now, by talking about systems and how we could work together going forward, I've managed to get her onto a monthly subscription. The job turned from that initial £300 for a one-off job to about £700 a year. So I more than doubled the fee for that particular client."

For Tina, although the fees involved aren't huge, what matters is that she now has the confidence to be upfront about charging her clients.

"I'm not shy anymore! I'll just say, this is my fee for this work. I recently set somebody up for a new company on Companies House and I was very clear that he had to sign my terms of engagement and put the money into my bank account before I did the job. I'm not prepared to take risks anymore. It's not just about pricing; it's about the whole method of getting in the work and then delivering it.

Another example is taking a phone call where the person wanted me to do some work for his company. I listened, agreed to do the work and then boldly said "we haven't discussed fees yet – how about X per day plus expenses?" he agreed, the terms of engagement were set up and sorted. Previously I would have put the telephone down, worried about how much to quote and dithered!"

CHAPTER TWO

Busting the myths

There are many myths around pricing – all of which need busting. In this chapter I am going to share with you four of the biggest myths that I see around pricing.

Myth 1 – Clients are price sensitive

The first and perhaps the biggest one, is that clients are price sensitive. When I do seminars and workshops I often ask the audience to raise their hand if they have price sensitive clients. Every time pretty much every single hand in the room goes up.

I then go on to say to them, "You are wrong, you do not have price sensitive clients".

What do I mean by that?

I mean that you have to understand what a price sensitive client looks like. Of course there are price sensitive people in society. In fact, behavioural economists estimate it's about 20% – i.e. that 1 in 5 people are price sensitive.

Let me describe a type of price sensitive person. Picture a little old retired lady who's got plenty of time on her hands. Every weekend she meticulously goes through the free newspapers armed with a pair of scissors cutting out coupons for money off her grocery shopping. She is price sensitive. She has time on her hands and so price is the sole thing she concentrates on as she is cutting out the vouchers. She is not your ideal client. If she is, perhaps you need to rethink your client base.

Instead have a think about your clients right now. How many of your clients own an Apple product – such as an iPhone, iPad or iMac? Any that do by definition are not price sensitive because there are cheaper phones, tablets and computers than those with the Apple logo on them.

Now think about your clients buying habits when it comes to coffee. How many of them buy their coffee from places like Starbucks or Costa Coffee? I would guess the majority. Once again by definition they cannot be price sensitive because there are cheaper ways that they could get their caffeine fix.

So your clients are not price sensitive. What they are is value sensitive, and they are two very different things.

I am guessing you, the reader, are also value sensitive. I imagine, for example, that you are not currently wearing the cheapest underwear that you could find? You are probably not driving the cheapest car you could find. You are also unlikely to be living in the cheapest house in the cheapest part of town, because for you value is more important than simply just price.

What we want is a bigger profit on the deal. The reason why people buy Apple products is because in their opinion the value they get from an iPhone, for example, is so much greater than the price they pay. So, whilst price is an important part of the value equation, it's not the only part.

Unfortunately, because we think clients are price sensitive, we focus on price. When we present our quotes and our proposals we try to be competitive compared with the firm down the road because we are desperate to win the business. We think that price is the most important thing, and it's not, it's value.

We need to start changing our focus to be around the value to the customer. We will look at that in more detail in steps two and three of the framework I will be sharing with you.

Myth 2 – You have to price low in a poor economy

Another of the common myths is that you have to price low in a poor economy. That could mean recessionary times or it could be that you are in an area of the country where it is more economically challenged.

Yet the reality is, and I have seen this from benchmarking studies that I have done in the UK, that very often firms of accountants and bookkeepers have got great prices even though they are in challenged areas.

Similarly, I have seen accounting and bookkeeping firms successfully increase their prices despite the fact that they are in the middle of a big recession. The fact of the matter is that when people say to me, *"I can't put my prices up because I'm not in the capital of the country, I'm not in London"* or, *"I can't put my prices up because we're in difficult times"* then they are just excuses. When you understand how to price then you can always get better results regardless of the circumstances.

Myth 3 – Being cheap wins you more clients

I am amazed that most accounting firms are obsessed by growth – it's all about, *"How many clients can we get?"* Well, that's not the key to profitability. In fact, what is interesting is that being cheap doesn't win you more clients necessarily.

I've already illustrated that with the Apple and Starbucks examples. Apple is expensive, and yet just look at its growth in market share in the last few years. If you think about Starbucks, the most profitable coffee shop on the planet, it is on every street corner in many of the major cities, and yet it's expensive.

Very often being more expensive wins you more clients.

If you're too cheap you will lose the best clients. Here's an example to illustrate why...

Why being cheap loses you clients

I am amazed how many accounting firms share their prices on their website and will offer to do accounts, tax returns, all the statutory work for a corporate business for between £300 to £500. That's ridiculously cheap.

They assume this will win them new clients. Instead what will happen is this. A good quality potential client looks at the accounting firm's website. This could be an ambitious business owner who is running a successful limited company – quite likely your ideal client. They see a ridiculously cheap price and instantly assume that because the price is so low the quality must be poor. They end up going somewhere else. If you're cheap you will be seen as being lower quality, and whilst that might attract some clients, it won't attract the right clients.

Myth 4 – Fixed prices equals value pricing

This is prevalent. I said earlier that now most accountants and bookkeepers recognise the need for the profession to move away from-time based billing. They recognise the need for value pricing.

Yet what I am seeing over the last 10 years is a huge shift towards giving fixed prices. People seem to think moving to fixed pricing is value pricing, it's not, they are two very different things, and let me explain why.

Let's say that you do a tax return, and you charge for a tax return at £500. When I ask an accountant or a bookkeeper, "*Why is £500 your fixed price?*" the answer is usually, *"Well we've looked at how long it takes to do historically and £500 is a good approximation based on the amount of time it will take to do this piece of work"*.

So whereas in the past the accountant or bookkeeper billed on the exact number of hours they spent, what they are now doing is estimating how long a job will take and giving the client a fixed price upfront.

And yet there is no link whatsoever between how many hours spent doing the piece of work and the value to the customer. Fixed pricing is not value pricing.

Ron Baker has a wonderful way of expressing this; *"Fixed pricing is time-based billing in drag."*

So they are the four big myths I come across. In the next chapter I am going to look at what I see as being the biggest mistakes.

CHAPTER THREE

The three big mistakes

Having looked at the four biggest myths in the last chapter let's now move onto what I see as being the biggest mistakes accounting and bookkeeping professionals make with their pricing.

These three mistakes all centre around one common theme – not involving the client in the pricing process. This is a fundamental error. You absolutely must have a pricing conversation with the client, and that pricing conversation must take place face to face in person, or as we move into this ever digital world using virtual meetings, in an online meeting with a webcam.

You have to do that because until you meet and talk to the client you have no idea what they value. You have to understand what their wants, needs and pain points are since you can't even begin to value price until you have identified those things.

Mistake 1 – Publishing prices

I mentioned in the last chapter that many accounting firms, and some bookkeeping firms, are starting to put prices on their website. Because they want to use it to win business, they make sure the prices are low. As a result, they end up attracting the price shoppers and putting off the good quality businesses.

Similarly, they will publish prices in marketing material such as brochures and send them out. You can't do either because people need to understand the value first before you can reveal the price.

A mistake I often made in the mid-90s when my business was growing quickly was when I was meeting lots of potential new clients, I would impress them with the things that I could do for them, and then towards the end of the meeting they would ask the question; *"That sounds great Mark what will it cost?"* and I would say, *"Let me think about that, I will create a proposal and I will put it in the post"*.

Today that proposal is likely to arrive a little quicker via email but it's still a mistake because you lose control of the process.

Just think for a minute about quotes you have received through the post or via email for a job you want doing – perhaps for a gardener or decorator. When you receive that quote I bet the first thing you look for is the part that shows the price because that is one crucial factor you have been waiting on. It's that upon which your final decision will often be based.

So when you send a proposal by email or through the post to a prospective client you have met it doesn't matter how nicely packaged your proposal is or how well you explain the benefits, they will flick through it and look for the price. And, when they find that price, they will make an instant judgement based on that number which most of the time is likely to be, *"That's a bit more expensive than I was expecting"*.

If it's a prospective client the chances are you will never hear from them again. They simply go to their current accountant or bookkeeper, or another of your competitors, and say, *"I have just received this quote, can you match or beat it?"* Your published price has become their bargaining tool.

So you must not send the price through the post because you lose control, you have to do the pricing with the client. Now, how do you do that? Well that is what we will look at when I take you through the formula.

Mistake 2 – Not giving clients certainty

The second big mistake is not giving clients certainty. One of the things I have learnt over the years is that when customers buy something there are two things they want; and one of those is certainty. The second I'll reveal shortly in the next common mistake.

They want certainty over what they get and what that price is going to be. The problem with the old fashioned way of pricing, billing based on the hour, is that the client doesn't get that certainty. They don't know what the price will be until the job is completed and the hours are added up and clients hate that.

You would hate it too. You want to know when you buy something exactly what the price is going to be right up front so you can plan, you can budget. So you must do that, you must give a price up front. Now you might be thinking, *"Yes Mark, but in the last chapter you said that fixed pricing is not value pricing"*; correct. But value pricing nevertheless does give certainty.

Mistake 3 – Not giving customers choice

The third big mistake stems from the second thing that all customers want besides certainty – choice. We are all individuals and we like to choose what we get. The problem with the way that we have packaged our solutions in the past is that it's a one-size-fits-all solution. We've tended to price on a standard hourly rate that everybody pays. When they ask for their accounts to be done they all get the same end result too – a few sheets of paper with a profit/loss account and a balance sheet.

But, every client is not the same, they are all individuals, they have different needs, different wants, different pain points, and so you must give them choice. I'll share how in a couple of chapter's time.

So those are the three big mistakes that I see over and over again. What I am going to do in the next chapter is talk more about why I think that the current times we are living in are exciting and a huge opportunity.

CHAPTER FOUR

Why today's opportunity is in the cloud

I entered the accounting profession way back in 1988. That is nearly 30 years ago. During those three decades I have seen a lot of change.

In the UK I have seen decreasing audit thresholds. Back in 1988 every limited company had to have an audit. Yet today in the UK, audit work has pretty much disappeared for the vast majority of accounting firms.

In the 1990s we saw self-assessment come to the UK, which completely changed the process for doing tax returns. We have seen many, many other changes to legislation, opening up the opportunity for new service offerings, for example.

We have also seen the huge rise of the Internet and that has had big implications on the way that we interact with clients. We have also seen the rise of social media over the last few years.

Both have completely changed the way that we market accounting and bookkeeping firms and are much more powerful than the marketing tools I had at my disposal when I was growing my accountancy practice back in 1996. Social media in particular is incredibly powerful for marketing accounting and bookkeeping firms and you need to get on that bandwagon.

However, despite all those big changes that I have seen, the single biggest change is that which is currently taking place – ***the move to cloud accounting***.

In the cloud both software and data sit on a server somewhere externally. In essence cloud accounting simply means the software and your clients' data are stored on someone else's computer. This is a much more secure environment than being run on an individual desktop.

That has big implications because it means that you can now work with your clients in real time. With their permission you can log in to their systems and get access to their numbers. You can see what their sales are for this month, what their debtors or accounts receivable are, or see what their profit for the last six months is.

You can access all that information anytime you want. In fact, with some systems you can even get it flagged up at your end when something hits a certain threshold. If, for example, a particular expense you have chosen to monitor goes over a predetermined level, such flagging will enable you to pick up the telephone and have a conversation with the client to see what is going wrong and if there is any way you can help.

A great phrase I hear over and over again is when accountants and bookkeepers tell me that it's a more *collaborative approach*.

So the reason why I think cloud accounting is the single biggest change I have seen in almost 30 years is because it completely changes the way we interact with clients. This is a huge opportunity.

Of course it is also a threat – especially since cloud accounting systems are automating much of the data processing. In fact, many leading universities have done studies to show that in the next few years about 95% of everything that accountants and bookkeepers traditionally do, will be completely automated. That is not that far-fetched. We are already seeing that happening.

With cloud accounting systems we are seeing bank feeds that automatically transfer bank transactions straight into the accounting system. We are seeing tools like Receipt Bank that enable the client to take a photograph of their cash receipts, for example, with their smart phone and it automatically posts them to the right place in their accounting system.

So cloud accounting is fundamentally changing the data entry part of the equation. But that's also an opportunity because if cloud accounting technology is reducing the amount of time to do the data processing, it frees us up to spend more time doing what we really should be doing, which is adding value, helping the client interpret their numbers, and helping the client to build a better, more successful business.

Cloud accounting has a number of tools that enable us to do that. For example, QuickBooks Online (QBO) has some amazing report functionality. You can create custom reports that include so much powerful data, or you can plug in third party applications that do management reports.

However, here is the big thing, to tap into the opportunity of cloud accounting we must also change our pricing model, because what cloud accounting does is it makes everything so much faster.

We can produce management accounts that used to take days or weeks at the touch of a button. If we price based on how long a job takes we will end up giving away all this powerful stuff, and yet just because it is now quicker and easier, the value has not changed. The value of management accounts, the value of management reports, and the value of the business advice that goes around it is immense and so you absolutely must figure out how to price that work based on the value to the customer and not how long it takes you to press that button and print out that report.

Cloud accounting fundamentally changes the relationship with the client. You can be more collaborative, more proactive and start to spend more time talking to the client, building the relationship and providing other services.

Those other services are what I came into the profession to do. I always wanted to make a difference to clients' lives. I didn't want to be forever reconciling bank accounts, and the great thing is there are some amazing software tools out there.

But it's not just the cloud accounting tools. There is also a complete holistic system that has been built up. In other words, different software providers are producing apps or tools that plug directly into cloud accounting systems that either help your client or help you.

There are apps that help clients with their cash collection, apps that help with stock control, apps that help with producing meaningful management information, and so on. Again that creates another opportunity for you. Because there are so many different plug-ins it is overwhelming from a business owner's point of view to know which stock control system they should use or which systems they should use to get paid quicker. When you become an expert and understand the marketplace, there is a huge opportunity that adds value by helping the client get onboard with cloud accounting and also build their whole infrastructure of other cloud tools that plug directly in.

So it's a big opportunity. It's also something that, whether you like the idea of the cloud or not, is already happening. Indeed I predict that in the not too distant future every single client will have to move onto the Cloud, because I believe that software companies will at some point stop supporting desktop systems.

When that happens your client's only other option is to run an Excel-based spreadsheet or a manual set of books and records that, as you know, is a crazy way to run the whole of the finance of your business. So everybody is going to have to move onto the Cloud at some point.

And that creates an opportunity for you. For every single client that you have that is currently not on a cloud accounting system, there is an opportunity for you to value price setting him or her up on the Cloud.

I recently hosted a webinar where I had just over 400 CPAs in the US. I asked the question, *"When you get the opportunity to move a client's records from, for example, a desktop system onto a cloud accounting system such as QuickBooks Online, how much do you price for that service?"*

What was interesting was 39% said they do it for free. They don't charge. Most of the rest said they charged less than $500. I asked the same question a couple of weeks before to another 400 or so CPAs and got similar results. I asked the same question in the UK too.

What I find over and over again is that somewhere between 35% and 50% of accountants and bookkeepers will set a client up on a cloud accounting system for free, and yet there is value in doing that.

If there is value then we should charge. Of the firms that are charging for that service, in almost every case, it's again a ridiculously low price because as an industry we haven't recognised the difference that we are making, the value that we bring to the table, by enabling a shift to the Cloud.

Inspiring stories

So what I want to share with you in the rest of this chapter are four powerful stories of firms who are already doing this, who are now systemising moving their clients to a cloud accounting environment, and in the process are starting to get significant prices.

In fact, one of my favourite stories is Sophia Botchway who, just like many other firms that I have worked with, is now charging over £1,000 (the equivalent of over US$1,500) every time for moving clients onto a cloud accounting system.

Clients are willingly paying the price because they can see the value. So just imagine the opportunity, think about how many clients you currently have who aren't at the moment on a cloud accounting system. If you were to multiply that number by £1,000 if you are in the UK or $1,500 if you're in the US, then that's the size of the opportunity for you; that's the quantum of the additional fees and profit from this particular service, when you understand how to properly value price it.

Then add on all of the prospective clients you could sign up in the next few years who are not currently on a cloud accounting system. This is a big opportunity for you.

So let's now look at those four stories.

How cloud accounting changed everything

Kay Westmorland runs Conscious Accounting as a sole practitioner. After 15 years as FD of the family business she is now working as a bookkeeper and management accountant by experience and has been running her practice since 2009.

If there's one thing guaranteed to make an accountant nervous, it's increasing prices. Many practices are reluctant to put up their prices by even a small percentage, fearing that clients will immediately desert them for a cheaper service.

That was exactly how Kay Westmorland felt. She had been charging the same price – £25 per hour – ever since she set up her practice in 2009. And she found it difficult to make progress. "Charging on an hourly rate or a day rate rather than per service was a real challenge," she says. "Knowing how to pitch my services so that people could see the value was really hard when I couldn't say exactly how much it was going to cost."

But Kay found that cloud accounting opened up a new way of doing things. Using Mark Wickersham's cloud accounting resource she began to offer a tiered level of service. "With a three-star, four-star or five-star service as the level goes up, the number of services you include increases and the price increases. Instead of having to pitch "I'll come and do it for you, but I'll charge you by the hour," my clients are very clear on what exactly I am offering and what they are going to pay for it."

In fact, the first time Kay used the cloud accounting resource (i.e. brochure) she gained a new client. "I'd been in my new office for about nine months and had a floor banner with the logo of the cloud software I use. The MD of a local software company from the office opposite passed my door one day and said, "Oh, you use that cloud accounting software – do you work for them?" I said, "No, I'm a management accountant. I help people transfer from other accounting systems to the cloud." He said, "Oh, I'd love to do that, I've been looking at it. I signed up for a free trial but I don't know where to start. Would you come and do that for us?"

"I went along and demonstrated the software and the benefits to the other Director. We hadn't really fixed which level of service he was going to go for so as the conversations progressed he said, "You've mentioned the credit control in the five-star service, what does that include? I've got some bad debts – would you be able to help me deal with those?" So, not only has he gone for the five-star service, which is £89 per month for 12 months, but he also wants to engage me to do some credit control for him. In the past I would have maybe charged him £200 – £400 and now I've got a contract that's well over £1,000, which is amazing. That was the first time I used it, so I'm thrilled – absolutely thrilled."

Using the brochure and the tiered pricing structure has helped Kay's practice enormously. "It makes it so much easier to market my services and to win business because it's a very clear process and I've actually got something that I can give people so they can make an educated choice based on the level of service that they want. It's turned a very intangible £25 per hour into something where the client can see what they'll get for their money."

The key learning points:

- Make sure you have a brochure for each of your services that offers three, four and five star levels. When you get into a conversation with a prospect you don't have to say, "Do you want to buy or not?" you can say, "Which level of service are you looking for?"

- Fixed prices mean that you know much more clearly where your cashflow is coming from and it helps your clients too, particularly if they are happy to pay in monthly instalments.

New technology and a new pricing strategy led to a 70% increase in fees

K. Phelan & Co. Ltd. was established in 2010 by Kieran Phelan. He works with a team of four and has around 150 clients.

When Kieran Phelan started his own practice he knew he was offering something new to businesses in Northern Ireland – cloud accounting – and that focusing on that was a way to differentiate himself from his competitors.

But although he was very forward thinking with cloud technology, when it came to pricing he found it hard to break old habits.

"For the first few months we even used timesheets!" he says. "And when we stopped timesheets, a lot of our prices were still based on what existing clients were paying so they weren't really any better. Because we wanted our clients to move onto the cloud and it was all pretty new, we wouldn't charge anything for setting them up and supporting them. I felt I couldn't ask them to pay for something I wanted them to do, even though it had great benefits for them."

Meanwhile, Kieran had been finding out about value pricing and became more and more convinced that it was the right thing to do. "I understood the concept, why it's needed and why we needed to go in that direction, not just for ourselves but for our clients too. By this time I was a couple of years into my practice and I had two team members so I knew that if we carried on pricing the way we had been we'd run out of cash quite quickly. The trouble was that I couldn't grasp the practicalities of how you actually do value pricing!"

While he knew he was undercharging a lot of his clients, he didn't want to simply raise his prices without being able to show that he was offering them something different. "So we drew up a list of all our resources, we redesigned our website and we came up with different packages for sole traders, partnerships, companies, charities etc. Within each package we designed various plans so there's the *Essentials Plan*, the *Plus Plan*, the *Power Plan*, but based on Mark's advice, we didn't show any of the prices on the website. We wanted to start pricing each and every customer individually."

Over the next few months, Kieran contacted his clients to offer them the new packages and the new prices. While a quick phone call was enough for some, others needed a sit-down meeting.

"It was time consuming, but it was very rewarding at the end of it," Kieran says. "The beauty of this process was getting our clients to understand what we really do for them. They started to understand how we save them tax, for example. So it was a great exercise in helping us to get the client to understand, and helping us to improve our communication skills – with the result of getting our prices up."

What Kieran realised in the course of these meetings was that different clients valued different things. So while the outline package was the same for everyone, the details of what he offered – and the price – were tweaked according to the needs of each client.

He tried the new approach with a long-standing client who quibbled every year over even a small fee increase. "I said, we're putting everybody through this cloud system and here are the benefits of the different packages that you can have for your company. I had to explain to him the Companies Act applications, the Section 419 applications and once we went through all that and I showed him how we avoided him having to pay certain types of taxes and the benefits he gained, he agreed to £1000 for setting up the cloud accounting system and a 33% increase on his fees. This was a guy who was squabbling over 3%!"

By running the exercise with 30 of his existing clients, Kieran managed to increase his fees by an average of 70%, adding £13,000 to his turnover.

Next he turned his attention to new clients.

"We had lost quite a few prospects while we were so swamped doing a lot of work for people and getting under paid for it, but now that I knew how to price and get paid for it, I started saying, 'Listen, can I come and see you now and show you we how we do things?' Based on our new resources and the cloud accounting proposal, I went out and got another dozen or so new clients. A number of them signed up for the cloud accounting system, which meant an extra £5,000. And all those new clients signed up for compliance work so that was another £10,000 a year of recurring fees. So we had £13,000 just from price increases, £5,000 for one off accounting systems set up, £10,000 for new compliance work and just having the confidence to go out and do it. So all in all, that added £28,000 to the top and bottom lines immediately."

And one client in particular stands out for Kieran. "This was the one where I knew the money I was getting paid was just ridiculously low, but the client was under cashflow pressure and I was afraid they wouldn't take it very well if I pushed for an increase. But we were doing so much for them – consolidated accounts every month, P&L balance sheets and a rolling cashflow forecast every month. The business just kept getting bigger and bigger and faster and faster and I just kept servicing them like a hamster on a wheel. They were paying under £1,000 per month for that service.

"Eventually I sat down with them with a new proposal. I gave them three options – either an Essential Plan with basic stuff and some reports every month. Or the middle package with nearly everything they needed. Or the top package with everything I was currently doing but with a new price of nearly £2,000 a month.

"They said to me that they couldn't do without me and immediately agreed to pay it. Out of the overall £28,000 increase in fees that client alone has added £11,500."

Kieran has now recruited another part qualified accountant to join his team so he can spend more time networking and running workshops and other events.

"I used to dread having that meeting about prices. I used to walk in and expect to end up fighting to get a price out of this person but now I say, 'look, here are your options, here's how we can do things for you.' I'm confident that we actually do good work for people and I'm not afraid to ask for more money for that."

The key learning points:

- Communicate the right message in the right way. Find out what matters to them, what's keeping them awake at night and then explain how you can save them that pain. Explain it in a way that means something to them and demonstrate it with actual results. Find out what they value most and then have the confidence to charge a decent price for it.

Less work, more time and more money – great result!

Sophia Botchway is the founder of Akusika Business Services. She has a team of three and is based in Oxfordshire.

Sophia Botchway didn't take the traditional route into accountancy. With a background in investment banking, then 12 years at the National Audit Office, she finally decided that it was time to make some money for herself and she set up Akusika Business Services in 2008. For the first three years she combined her own business with her job, but since 2011 she's been working full time for herself.

But it hasn't been easy. "I must say the beginning was really, really hard work" she says. "Like everyone else I was doing what I thought was the right thing to do. I knew I wanted to earn at least £30 an hour so my practice was based on charging per hour to most of my clients. And again, I was doing all the work and then sending out an invoice and waiting for the money to come in."

One of the options Sophia offered her clients was cloud accounting. As an incentive to sign up with her, she would give away a cloud accounting package for free along with her bookkeeping service. However, she found that although most clients took up the offer, they weren't actually using the software and she would end up adding the data herself.

"I was putting in an awful lot of hours working evenings and weekends and I was constantly tired, but I wasn't really seeing much return. I kept thinking maybe I should go back to the NAO because I'm working a lot more hours for a lot less money!"

What changed things for Sophia was learning from Mark the concept of value pricing and how to offer different levels of service. With a brochure to explain her cloud accounting service and three pricing options, she tried the new approach with the next prospective client she met.

"I gave them some information and the brochure prices and that first client chose the premium package on the cloud! Straight away we had the top price, which worked out to be about £1500. We have since been using that consistently. No client gets free software anymore.

"What I've learned is that previously we weren't giving them the opportunity to make their own decisions. By giving the software to them for free they didn't actually value it. We were still doing all the work on it for them as well as paying for it – and it was costing us time. With the client choosing the package they want and owning it, they actually started using it, putting the transactions on themselves.

"So that saves us time as in effect they're doing the bookkeeping for us and we're just checking it over to make sure that they're charging things in the right way. It saves us time, we're making money from it and it's hassle free. Amazing!"

Sophia has offered the new packages to 20 of her clients so far – and has had a phenomenal 100% success rate. What's more, 19 have taken up the premium package, with only one opting for the basic level.

"I did have one client who decided not to go for our service because they thought we were expensive," Sophia says. "They had been offered a similar service for £70 per month, instead of the £277 we were charging. Three months later that same client came back. I had actually increased my prices slightly by then, but she accepted it anyway. The other accountant hadn't done any work for her at all in the three months so she could now see the value in coming to us."

The key learning points:

- Never, ever price on an hourly rate – always price on the value the client is getting from you.
- Don't undercut your own prices. If the client is not willing to pay your price, they're not the right client for you. That will stop other accountants always trying to under-price each other, which damages the industry.
- Use GoCardless – it's the most amazing invention ever! It collects all our payments on the first of each month so it's better for cash flow, we know what we've got coming in most of the time, we know when it's going to be in, how much it's going to be and we can actually provide a better service for our clients because we're not having to chase them for payment.
- Use Cloud Pricing software – Having to guess the price is as bad as hourly pricing. With the pricing software in front of the client, they can choose the services they want and can see exactly what they are paying for.

Moving to the cloud opens up big opportunities to price higher

Matt Harrison is the director of Calluna Tax Services Ltd in Northampton

Matt has moved one client from a fee of £150 per month to £1000 per month plus a one off payment of £1500 as a catch-up fee – without any objections from the client.

This remarkable story began when he took on the client to do their tax and accounts and moved them over to QuickBooks. Having access to their online data meant he was able see that after about six months they had stopped keeping their books up to date. A few months later he checked again and saw the situation hadn't improved. When he contacted them to see how they were managing (knowing, of course, that they weren't) they agreed to him bringing everything up to date and then looking after the books in future.

Using value pricing, Matt highlighted the need to bring the books up to date to meet the P11D deadline and explained that there would be a premium fee to fast track the work. "I gave them the option to pay the £1600 catch-up fee in three instalments or to pay a lump sum with £100 discount. They chose the second option and paid the next day," Matt says.

He then bundled together the tax, accounts and bookkeeping work and offered the client different levels of service. He took the time to explain exactly what he would be doing at each level and included added value services at the higher levels. "I also took the approach that the government's recent announcement of the abolition of the tax return meant that tax and accounts were becoming an all year round service, not just once a year. So I was selling an all round tax, books, accounts support package and not just accounts and tax return prep. I also tied regular preparation of management accounts into the fee."

Historically Matt would have charged around £280 per month for the work, but the client agreed to a fee of £1000.

CHAPTER FIVE

It's good to be small

In the last chapter I talked about why we are living in exciting times and the big opportunity of cloud accounting. I also think it's an exciting time for the smaller firms of accountants and bookkeepers, so if you are a firm with say five staff or less, or perhaps even a solo practitioner, then this chapter is for you.

You see if I go back ten or twenty years then everybody had ambitions to build a big firm. Largely that was down to the way that, particularly in the accounting profession, accounting firms are valued; based on a multiple of gross recurring fees. In other words, our annual fees.

Twenty years ago that multiple may have been 1.4 or 1.5 times the level of sales. But now that number is coming down and you'd be lucky to get 1 or 1.1 times the value of your sales. Of course that is assuming you can even find a buyer because now we are getting the baby boomers looking to retire, there are lots of people looking to sell accounting firms and not enough younger people who can afford to buy them out.

So because of that out-dated valuation model for professional accounting firms we had this fixation on needing to grow our accounting firms and be big; to *collect* clients, regardless of whether those clients are a good fit or not.

Bizarre!

I think times have completely changed; I think it is an exciting time for the smaller firm and there are a number of reasons for this. Firstly, I think that technology now makes it much easier for the smaller firm to compete with the larger firm because a lot of the mundane work, the data entry work, is being automated.

If we get to a stage where all the compliance work is automated, and we're fast going in that direction, then the services that we offer then become the value added services. It becomes things like business consulting, mentoring, services like tax planning, tax advice.

Many of these services are really about clients buying us; it is about the relationship. If you become good at your particular area of expertise, whether it's tax planning, business advice, profit improvement advice, setting people up on the Cloud, whatever it is, when you are the expert in that field then you are competing on a level playing field with the larger firms. They want to buy you and what you do... they don't want to buy what your firm does.

So technology is helping you. It's also meaning that you don't necessarily have to have a big infrastructure behind you. To be able to offer a wide range of services in the past you had to have nice offices and a team of people. Now much of what we do as an industry can be delivered through technology.

I am now seeing, for example, a number of smaller firms who are having meetings with clients either in hotel receptions or using tools like GoToMeeting or Zoom with a webcam. They don't need to have an expensive office.

That in turn opens up the market place beyond your local area. We no longer need an expensive office in every corner of the county or state to service more clients.

Technology is changing things, but we are also seeing the growth of outsourcing. This is not just the outsourcing of compliance work. The truth is most things can be outsourced now and we have seen the growth of websites such as Fiverr.com and oDesk where you can find people to do specific tasks for you.

You can have virtual assistants, you can outsource the answering of your telephone, you can outsource all of your graphic design work, and your marketing can be outsourced. In fact most things can be outsourced, which means that the smaller firms can now provide many more services without having to have all of the costs and the hassle of an in-house team.

The third big change that we are seeing, and we have seen over the last 100 years, is the changes to brands. If we go back 100 years ago it was all about corporate brands, for example, Coca Cola. Then we started seeing the branding shift towards products becoming a brand and so we think of things like the iPhone as a brand in itself. Yes, Apple is a great brand, but the iPhone is also a great brand in its own right.

We have seen the increasing importance of products becoming brands. But the more recent shift we have seen over the last 10 years or so is the increasing importance of personal brands. You think of Virgin and actually the more important personal brand is the man behind it – Sir Richard Branson. You think of Apple and you think of Steve Jobs.

Personal brands are much more important because people ultimately buy from people. People would much rather buy from a person they can relate to than a faceless corporate. The thing about the accounting and bookkeeping profession is that it is a relationship business. The reason why your clients are clients of your firm is because of you. Ultimately they buy you as a person, and they cannot buy you at the firm down the road.

I believe the smaller firm, and the solo practitioner (i.e. a solo practitioner is someone with no team members) for example, has a greater opportunity to offer that more personalised service that individuals often crave. Whereas the large mid-tier, and large multi-partner firms, can't necessarily offer that powerful personal touch because they are by definition largely the more faceless corporate brand.

So I think these three things – the change in technology, the ability to outsource pretty much anything, and the increasing importance of personal brands (and the ability with tools like social media to help us promote those personal brands) – mean that the smaller firm is now on a level playing field. They can now build a very successful and a profitable firm without having to be big.

And one of the interesting things I notice is smaller firms are getting to grips with value pricing much quicker. In contrast, large multi-partner firms are struggling with the change, often mired in tradition. No longer is it the case that larger firms command higher fees.

Smaller firms are becoming more profitable because they are small and consequently tapping into the opportunities presented by technology, outsourcing, social media and wrapping it all up in value pricing.

As you read the stories within this book, notice how many of them are small firms.

Your 7-step formula for implementing value pricing

In this book I have already shared some of my key thoughts on where we are as a profession but in the next few chapters I will take you through a 7-step formula – a structure that when you apply it to every pricing opportunity enables you to get much better results and build your profitable firm – whatever its size.

I will take you through each of the seven steps, and share with you stories to illustrate how firms have taken these ideas, these steps, and are getting much better prices, and becoming more profitable as a result.

Very often firms are getting prices not of 5-10% higher, but in some cases, double the price for doing essentially the same thing, and in some cases there are stories of firms getting four times the price. That's a 300% increase in price almost all of which falls to bottom line profit. When you master value pricing you have the ability to add tens of thousands to your bottom line profit.

So let's start with the first step in the next chapter.

CHAPTER SIX

STEP 1 —

Your price discrimination strategy

Price discrimination is simply the economists' label for *'charging different customers different prices'*.

Of all the steps I will share with you, charging different customers different prices is perhaps the most important. Here is a fundamental thing about value pricing. Each of your clients values things differently to everyone else. I mentioned that earlier in the book as one of the reasons why value pricing has always been seen as being something that is difficult to implement

This idea that different customers value things differently really is at the heart of value pricing. It means we have to figure out a price discrimination strategy. There are many different ways we can do this.

We come across all sorts of different price discrimination techniques in the marketplace. For example, if you are in the UK and want to get a train ticket to take you to London to arrive for 8.30am so you can be at your 9am business meeting, you will pay a higher price than if you catch a different train that will arrive at, let's say, 9.30am.

So if you're a tourist and it doesn't matter when you arrive in London, you can pay a lower price and arrive at 9.30am. But if you are a businessperson that absolutely must be in London for that 9am meeting you accept that you will pay a higher price.

In this instance the rail companies use time as one of the ways to discriminate to charge different customers different prices. We can use that same technique, and many more, in the accounting profession.

Rail companies use another technique; first class versus coach class. Some customers choose to pay a higher price because they perceive a greater profit to them (in terms of the gap between the benefit to them and the price they pay) of sitting in a first class carriage.

Menu pricing and the *Magic of Three*

However, what I want to focus on in this book is the one which is both the easiest to understand and also the most powerful for the accounting and bookkeeping professions; menu pricing. This is about giving people a choice of different bundles, options or packages.

Earlier in this book I explained why we must give choice, because clients are individuals and they have their own specific wants and needs. If you've read my first book, *'Effective Pricing for Accountants'*, I talked about menu pricing in there and the *Magic of Three*.

The *Magic of Three* simply means that when you create your packages you should always, unless you can prove otherwise through testing, create three options. Sometimes these are described as Bronze, Silver, Gold, for example, or 3-star, 4-star, 5-star. Let's not worry about the labels for just a moment.

There is some science and psychology behind the *Magic of Three* because what tends to happen is most people will choose the middle option since it is seen as being the safest option. That creates a big opportunity for you and your pricing therefore. For example, if you decide that you are sceptical about the idea of putting your prices up, then why not create three options and present them to your client.

You can make the entry-level option or the bronze level, the same package and price as you charged last year (perhaps plus an inflationary increase). Then create another option, a middle level, with some extra value and then create a premium higher priced option, and test the three.

What you will find is that some of your clients will *choose* to pay you more money because they see greater value in the middle option, or even the premium, most expensive option.

We see this in the world around us. All the most successful and profitable companies on the planet use menu pricing and use the *Magic of Three*. I've already mentioned Starbucks. When you go in for your coffee fix you will see, on the menu behind the counter, three choices of sizes.

Starbucks describe them as Tall (which is the small one strangely enough), Grande, and Venti. They are using the *Magic of Three* and recognise different customers value things differently.

Some people who perhaps are less thirsty or a little more price sensitive may choose the Tall. Then there are other people at the other end of the spectrum who see more value in the extra offered by the Grande or even the Venti. They will voluntarily – and eagerly – choose to take more money out of their pocket and pass it across the counter to Starbucks for that size option. Starbucks' profit just went up considerably.

For Starbucks that means millions added to bottom line profits – something that would be thrown away if all Starbucks ever offered its customers was just a Tall latte.

Menu pricing is the first step towards value pricing because by creating three different packages although the value is subjective, the customer – i.e. your client – will choose the package that, for them, best represents the most value. So by giving them those three choices they will self-select and choose the package that has components in there they value at a price that they can afford.

I have seen firms implement this one idea and they have reported back to me that just by giving people the choice they have increased their average prices across their entire firm by 20% or more. That price increase goes straight to bottom line profits, which for a typical accounting or bookkeeping firm, could equate to a 50% increase.

If you could increase your income by 50% over the next year, how would that make you feel? What could you do with that additional income?

Inspiring stories

What follows are the stories of four such firms that have already used menu pricing and achieved great results. They range from a sole practitioner to a start-up accounting firm and two larger firms and illustrate just how powerful menu pricing can be. Regardless of the size of your firm.

“Menu pricing meant my clients were happy to pay much higher fees than before”

Clear Accounting NI is based in Dundonald, near Belfast in Northern Ireland. It was started by Bill Ellison in 2014 and currently employs Bill and an accounts assistant. At the time of writing, the practice had around 100 clients.

In the summer of 2014, Bill Ellison had been in partnership with another accountant for five years in a practice with around 300 clients. But he was concerned that they were charging too little and had too many low level clients, most of them self-employed rather than business owners.

When he became aware of Mark Wickersham’s ideas on pricing, he knew that he had to make big changes to the way he was working.

“I began to realise that the practice I was in just wasn’t profitable. I was never going to be able to increase prices and move the business along while I was still involved in the partnership,” he says.

So Bill made the bold decision to set up on his own and Clear Accounting NI opened in October 2014. He brought some of his existing clients with him because he knew they were interested in growing their businesses. “Using cloud accounting software and applying some of Mark’s techniques I knew I could start doing much more in the way of bookkeeping and acting as a financial controller for some of my client companies. So since then I’ve started promoting the bookkeeping aspect and my income through bookkeeping now has gone up by about £700 or £800 a month.”

With more clients now coming on board for the bookkeeping service, Bill has been able to take on a trainee accounts assistant and this has freed up his time to do other work.

His other big success has come through menu pricing, particularly for incorporations. At his previous practice he would have charged £170 for a basic service, but now Bill offers three different levels of service. “The basic level is £375, the medium level is £575 and then the optimum level is £975. I’ve had three companies come to me recently for incorporation and two of them have gone for the medium level and one’s gone for the optimum level. So work that would have brought in £500 previously has now got me £2250.”

Bill is very clear about how he sees his role. “My idea of setting up an accountancy practice is shaped by my background in commerce and industry and the businesses I have owned in the past. My idea was always to act as a consultant or financial director for clients, but without the ability to price correctly and without the cloud accounting systems I was never able to do that. So this has given me the opportunity to do that and to help clients grow their businesses which is how I see my role as an accountant.”

The key learning points:

- Explain clearly what services you're offering. When the client understands what's involved and what you can do for them, they are far more likely to say 'yes' to you.
- Use menu pricing. Combined with a detailed explanation of your services this really makes a difference. The client feels in control of what it's going to cost them so they feel free to make their own decisions. And more often than not they go for the middle or highest option, not the lowest.

Building relationships to deliver more value

Iain Weir set up his practice, Weir Associates, in 2015 after working in industry for 20 years. He is based just south of Cambridge and is gradually building up his client base after starting with just two.

After 20 years in industry, Iain Weir decided that he'd had enough of working for other people and resolved to set up on his own. He realised that cloud accounting was making it easier than ever before to work virtually and to support clients without needing to take on a whole team of people. And right from the start he knew he wanted to do more than just compliance.

"It's about much more than just filing the accounts at the end of the year or doing the tax returns. It's about building a relationship and hopefully becoming more of a business partner and adviser to them to give them that extra value," he says.

Even so, when it came to pricing, Iain's strategy was to look at the fees of online accountants and price his services slightly cheaper. "People on the internet no doubt have teams of trainees just churning stuff out. Whereas I feel I can offer a lot more than that, certainly a lot more of a personal service and I'm certainly more available to go and see them. So I definitely priced myself too low."

But something Iain heard during one of Mark's presentations struck a chord. "Mark said if you just give somebody one price then you aren't giving them the opportunity to spend any more money with you. But when you give people three options it shows them that you can offer a whole range of services. So whether it's just the bare bones or whether they want you to get more involved and advise them more you're giving them that opportunity."

As a result, Iain put in place a three tier pricing strategy and increased his basic price. "My bare bones package is only about 10% more expensive than when I first priced it, but I am doing far less within that. What I originally included in that package is now nearer to the middle and top end ones. So those prices have increased by at least 50%, if not 60% or 70%."

Cloud accounting was what enabled Iain to set up his practice in the first place and he uses several different pieces of cloud-based software. But the ease of use and fast results have also highlighted a growing risk to traditional accountants.

"One client set up Xero themselves, so they had access to all their figures. So they said to me, 'Well, all you do at the end of the month is hit a button that produces the report.' And yes, you can do that and that's fine if you've got a bookkeeper and you just want a cash overview for your business. But whether you actually understand what you are looking at or whether you actually want proper accounting so you know what you'll be taxed on – that's completely different."

And that's made it more important than ever to make sure clients understand all the different ways Iain can help them.

"Before I probably would have just gone straight in and said, 'This is what you need to do and this is the single price that I am prepared to do it for you. And by the way, if you ever need some more help, let me know and we can talk about that when the need arises.' Then, if they ever came back to me I would then have to market those extra services to them. So maybe 18 months down the line when I came to do their accounts, I'd look at the figures and say, 'Oh, actually it looks like you've really been struggling. You could have done with some of my other services during the year.' Rather than really working with them from the start because they have seen what other services you can offer, and they've decided that they really need that."

Iain's approach to pricing has changed hugely since he started. "I don't really care what the competition think they're worth because I know that I am me and I know what I'm worth. And I've proved that people are willing to pay. It's having that sort of confidence and self worth to go out there and say this is how I operate. This is what I can offer you. And to be able to explain to the clients exactly what it is you are doing, what they are going to get and what it means. My prices are probably 50% higher than at the start and in the long term the goal is that it will lead to not needing so many clients. So now to reach my goals I don't need 100 clients, I only need 60 clients. Then I can spend more time on each one, building that relationship and hopefully building more profitable services because I am not getting paid just to do the donkey work."

The key learning points:

- The important thing is to give the client a choice and allow them to spend more money with you. Don't look at the competition. Don't look at what others are doing and copy it, because they are not you. Really talk to the client, don't just send information out to them, really explain to them what exactly you are going to do for them, what they are going to get, what are the outcomes and the effort that is involved in what you need to produce for them.

- Try to price the value to the client and use pricing discrimination. Some clients will be able to afford more than others. And just because you are providing the same or similar services to people don't be afraid of charging one sector more than another sector. Certainly when it comes to tax recovery or VAT recovery, think about giving a guarantee – 'If I am not successful, you don't pay me anything. But if I am you pay me 20%-30% of what I recover.' Because if you don't do that work the client has no benefit. If you do the work and you are successful the client can have a lot of money back in their pocket.

The huge difference value pricing made for this practice

Croucher Needham was established in 2007 in Bedford and now also has an office in Saffron Waldon. The practice has a team of 20 and turnover is around £1.3 million. The client base is mainly owner-managed businesses.

In 2014 James Marchant joined Croucher Needham from a background at a much bigger, Top 10 firm. Yet when it came to pricing, he found that the challenges were just the same.

"I was convinced we were giving away value," he says. "We were pricing on the traditional basis: hourly rates, making up a charge-out rate, making up what time we were going to post and then having an arm wrestle with the client about what we were going to write off. It wasn't nice for us, and it wasn't nice for our clients either – nobody liked doing it."

What's more, James felt that as well as the compliance work they were doing, they were actually providing an advisory role but were simply giving away their expertise for free. He was certain that value pricing was the answer to the problem.

Working with AVN, James began to introduce a three tier pricing structure using the Time's Up! software. "That takes it so far and that's helpful when you're doing compliance work," he says.

"But the challenge for me was how to use three tier pricing in an advisory work scenario."

What he did was to develop a system that worked equally well for compliance or advisory work.

"I start by making a promise to clients that we will always agree the fee and the scope of the work in advance before any work starts. And I regularly use those words as a frame of reference when I go to the client with proposals. 'I have made you the promise. Let me go away, come up with some scope and some pricing and then we can go through that and decide what works best for you.' We badge that three tier pricing as Essential, Full and Premium and that's consistent whether it be compliance work or advisory work – we try and always break things down in that way."

While scoping advisory work wasn't easy at first, James has found that it's become easier with practice and he's now able to come up with discussion points quite quickly. And when pricing each level the starting point is now always the value to the client.

"It's very easy when it's a tax saving opportunity because the figures are there in black and white. It's not so easy when it's advice about a particular project, but we always try and think about what's in it for the client. What are we saving them in terms of time, money, hassle? What are we giving them in terms of peace of mind? When it comes to pricing tax work we always try and go in at a price of 25% of the tax saving we're making."

Over the past 12 months James has worked on five research and development tax claims for three clients, generating a total of £98,000 in tax savings. "We have been paid fees of £22,758 so that works out about 23%. In the past I would probably have done those on an hourly rate basis so it would have worked out about £2,000 a claim, maybe £10,000 in total fees. So it's a big difference from £10,000 to nearly £23,000."

James now also agrees a time frame for payment, so they get paid as they go along. "I've been there and seen it before: you do the work, agree the fee afterwards and then you wait until the client feels ready to pay you which is never a nice place to be because you've already delivered all the value. So, again as part of agreeing the scope we make it very clear how much we are going to get paid and over what time frame."

This made a big difference with one client in particular.

"A client wanted some advice on merging two subsidiary businesses within his group. And the conversation opened with, 'James, can you give me some pros and cons on merging these two companies?' In the past I would probably have dived straight in, started giving away all the value and then thought to bill him for a few hours of time after the event. I would have been lucky to get a fee somewhere between £750 to £1000 and I would have felt fine with it. He's a difficult client as well. But I stuck to the promise we make and the three tier system so option 1 was simply to identify all of the key issues that he needed to think about; that was two instalments of £597.

"Option 2 was all that plus identifying all his actions, meeting with him and his stakeholders throughout the project, timetabling it, doing the project plan, doing a financial analysis of the differences and identifying the tax factors. That was going to be four instalments of £897.

"And then option 3 was all of the above plus mocking up some financials for the newly merged business, identifying some key merger cost savings and arranging to get the legal documentation drafted for the merger as well. And that was going to come in at a grand price of £7,688. And all of those were going to be paid over four months. To my delight the client went for the third option, our Premium package. I would have billed in the past somewhere between £750 and £1000 so it's a massive, massive difference for us."

While James feels they haven't done everything they could with value pricing, he's confident that they are well on their way. His other partners are fully on board and they have started to roll out Direct Debits to all their clients. "Even though it's early days, at the last count we had something like £6,000 a month coming in on Direct Debit and I can only see that improving as we go forward."

And the future looks bright.

"Being very conservative, I've identified £100,000 worth of additional fees across the practice'" he says. "It's a big number for us. Beyond that, what's absolutely clear is that when you are talking to potential clients they love the proposition. They get it from the off: 'my accountant doesn't do this. This is really great'. Just handing them the iPad to be able to play with the pricing themselves is a great step. It's much more transparent and less of an embarrassing conversation. It's just, 'OK, let's have a look what's here, you pick and mix if you like as much as you want to.' I feel really comfortable now. It's just part of the way I do business."

The key learning points:

- The number one thing that clients don't like is big surprises. So make the promise to your client upfront that you are always going to give them a price. Sometimes that means that you won't be able to give them the price straight away and you'll have to go away and think about what all the options are. So that's a change of approach from the start.

- Make sure you do invest the time to scope the work properly. What you are doing is transitioning the heartache and the challenges of having a fee battle down the line to giving the client absolute clarity upfront and actually giving yourself a better opportunity of getting a much higher fee. Accept that you're going to have to invest time upfront. But as you get more confident and more experienced, the time you have to invest will become less and less.

- Turn off that old mindset of thinking 'How long is it going to take me time-wise multiplied by my charge out rate?' Absolutely stop it and instead think, 'What's the value for the client here? Am I taking away hassle, am I taking away pain, am I generating tax savings?' I typically include a guarantee around my R&D (Research and Development) tax claims so if I'm not successful you don't pay me. It takes away the barriers. I back myself to make sure that I get the refund for the client.

Using psychology to boost profits and keep clients happy

Walji & Co. is a two partner practice based in Eastleigh, Hampshire. Founded over 30 years ago it has a team of six client managers and a client base of around 150.

As a long-established practice, Walji & Co. has well-planned systems and processes for both the compliance work and the advisory work it does. But partner Reza Hooda has still found ways to innovate, making the practice more profitable and bringing in new clients.

"Mark has really made us aware of the psychology involved in pricing and that's helped us to price our work more effectively and gain a better understanding of how buyers make decisions. It's all about how to package and price every element of what we do; in particular the power of three has been highly beneficial in putting together our packages."

Reza has found that offering three levels of service works equally well for compliance and advisory work. "I would never have thought of doing that before for advisory work. I would have just said, 'OK, this is the work that I've been asked to do, these are the brochures and packages, this is the value you'll get as a client, the price will be x.' But having understood the buying psychology from Mark's sessions, it's all about pulling that into three packages and giving the client three options. I can now say to the client, 'you're always getting value, but you're getting different levels of value based on these three options.' So I can upsell what ordinarily I would have just provided one price for. And I'm giving the buyer the control and responsibility over which package they go for, and that means there is more likelihood of getting a positive result."

This strategy helped Reza when he was approached for some tax advice over the sale of several businesses.

"Initially we did a review and commissioned a report and the client then asked us to quote for implementing it. So I thought I'd put Mark's advice into action and come up with three options for the client. I worked out a base price for the minimum level of service that he would need to implement the plan then I managed to find additional layers of value that we could bring in to give a middle and a premium option. On top of that I included an option for an additional amount per month payable upfront to cover any queries arising from a future investigation by HMRC. If there's no HMRC inquiry then it's total profit.

"We're not the client's accountant at all, this was just a bespoke advisory piece of work. So I pulled that all together, came up with the three packages and sent it to the client. He sat on it for a while, but in the end he came back to me and said yes and to my surprise, he actually went for the premium option with the extra bolt-on, the maximum that I quoted for. In total that piece of work is worth £8,500 which he will pay over four months. At base level it would have been £3,000-4,000, so the end result is a 100% uplift."

Reza has also had great success with pricing software, particularly when it comes to bookkeeping work. "Whereas previously we would just have the accounting year-end meeting, now with the software we're able to say, 'we can take on the bookkeeping headache for you too, would you like us to quote?' Then we can do the quote there and then and instantly give them an idea of what the outlook is. We've gained additional work from several clients in this way."

The key learning points:

- Understand your prospects. Accountants are in the service business, just like coffee shops or the insurance industry, and understanding the psychology of buying is very important.
- Use the rule of three. It really works.

CHAPTER SEVEN

STEP 2 —

Providing a better solution to your clients

Once you have figured out what your three packages are going to be you need to think about what more you can do to give the client a better solution before you present those packages to your client.

This is a must. I believe that as a profession our primary focus should always be on how we can add as much value to our clients as possible. We should be focused on changing people's lives, because we're in a very privileged position as a profession. As accountants and bookkeepers we are able to get access to all of our client's financial data whenever we want. Thanks to our ability to access that information we also have the ability to provide advice to help that client improve their business, their results and ultimately their lives.

Remember that brilliant book I referenced earlier by Steve Pipe, called *'The world's most inspiring accountants'*. It is packed full of stories of accountants who have quite literally changed people's lives.

You can do that too.

This ability to change lives should be our number one focus because it's the right thing to do. But if we are to evolve as a profession it's also something we have to do. As we have already discussed, compliance work is dying and data entry is being automated. We have to start doing different things and start doing more things for the client. We have to start making a difference to people's lives.

But how do you add more value?

I believe that with every service you offer there is always something more that you can do. So the first thing to be aware of is that when we are looking at the benefits of what we do there are two distinct types. There is what I call the 'tangible benefit' – i.e. the physical product you create. For example, in the case of a tax return preparation, it's the tax return itself.

Here you can look at what other tangible things you can do to add more value. For example, if you wanted to make your annual financial statements more valuable you could provide a benchmarking report showing the client how their business compares to other similar businesses in their industry.

But don't overlook the second type of benefit – the intangible benefit. The intangible benefit is the service wrapper that sits around what you're offering. It's the customer experience and includes things like the speed of response and the speed of delivery. It includes things like the level of person doing the work.

For example, if they are dealing with a partner in an accounting or bookkeeping firm, then by their very seniority such staff are perceived to be greater value than if the client was dealing with the most junior member of the team.

Think about how to give your customers a better experience. Understand what things are important to them but also realise the importance not just of what you do but also how you do it and how you deliver it.

A great way of doing this is to have a brainstorming session where you think about what else you can do to give more value to your clients. Involve your entire team in the brainstorming session, that way you'll come up with many more ideas.

When you are working on pricing a specific request from a client you must ask the question, "*What does the client really want here?*"

For example, imagine a client comes to you and says, *"Can you prepare a cash flow forecast for my business?"* You tell them you can, go ahead and do it but you fail to ask ***why*** they want it. The problem is what the client wants or needs aren't often the same as the words that come out of their mouth.

Instead, in the face-to-face meeting you need to ask why they want a cash flow forecast preparing. Their reply could be along the lines of, *"Because I need to get finance from the bank to buy a new piece of machinery that will make my business much more efficient and the bank manager said I needed to get a cash flow forecast from my accountant"*.

So you might then say, *"Okay, great and just out of interest what impact will that piece of machinery have on your business?"* and the client replies, *"Well, this will increase my efficiency so much I will add £50,000 to my bottom line profit every year as a result"*.

Finally you've understood the end result of the cash flow forecast and realised that what you are doing is not just creating a cash flow forecast but helping them to acquire something that will add £50,000 to their bottom line. That's the real value of what you are doing.

Now armed with the understanding of why the client needs the cash flow forecast and the result that will give them you can now turn your thinking to, *"What can I do to help them get that piece of machinery? What can I do to help them generate that additional £50,000 of profit every year?"*

And now you start coming up with the ideas that really help. You might offer to accompany the client to the meeting with the bank manager to help interpret the numbers and therefore help get that bank finance your client so badly wants.

There may be other options too. Through your knowledge of the industry you might be aware and have access to alternative forms of finance or know of grants or have a grant finding solution. There are many things that we can do to give the client more. These are just a few ways you may be able to better help your client simply by asking why they need what they have asked for.

Adding value with your cloud accounting solutions

We have already looked at the power of cloud accounting. QuickBooks Online, for instance, is a wonderful cloud accounting tool that enables you to add more value by having access to the client's information in real time.

Here are just a few examples of additional things you can do to add more value and give a better solution:

- Monitoring critical expenses in real time and giving proactive advice when they exceed predetermined levels

- Regular management reports
- Regular meetings where you provide business advice and help the client interpret their numbers
- Real time monitoring of debtors (accounts receivable) and advising the client on cash collection
- Advising on and installing other cloud tools which integrate with their cloud accounting solution

In other words, rather than just doing the bookkeeping or annual financial statements you are instead offering more value – perhaps as part of your premium package offer.

Many of these additional things are high value but do not require much time to deliver. For example, with a cloud accounting system you can create high impact reports at the touch of a button. And even meetings, which used to be time consuming, can now be done online – eliminating travel time – using tools such as Zoom, GoToMeeting or Skype.

All these things are highly valuable and will command a premium price.

Inspiring stories

Once again I have two success stories to illustrate my point. These are two very forward thinking accountants who focused on adding value with great impacts on both their clients and their own results.

"By focusing on value to the client rather than just compliance we are now able to charge 150% more than we would have done previously."

Karl Roberts is a partner at GMR Accountants Ltd., based in Southport, Merseyside. The practice has three partners plus 8 team including part time employees and approximately 300 – 350 clients.

Set up by two partners in 1981, GMR Accountants operated as a traditional accountancy practice. And billing for jobs in the traditional way meant that they often waited for six or even nine months before they were paid.

When Karl Roberts became a partner in 2012, he was full of new ideas and passionate about driving the business forward. "Becoming a partner changed the way I think, from an accountant to a business owner," he says. So finding out the scale of debtors came as a shock.

The practice wanted to move away from pure compliance work and start adding value to the services they offered. They reasoned that clients would be willing to pay higher fees if they were getting something they really valued, not just a set of accounts and a tax bill at the end of the year. But initially Karl lacked the confidence to make any changes. "I looked at my partners who've been doing this for 30 years and thought, I can't charge as much as them because I'm not as good as them," Karl says now. "As a new partner I wanted to bring something to the table by getting in new clients. So to get prospects to say 'yes' I used to go in at a cheap price."

But Karl was beginning to understand that there was another way. Watching Mark Wickersham's pricing videos and then becoming a member of AVN showed him that other accountants were doing things differently.

Karl had taken on a new client, a tiling contractor who also ran a tile shop, and had turnover of £300,000 – £400,000. In the first year he charged the same fee as the previous accountant, but in the second year, after taking on board Mark and Steve Pipe's messages about value pricing and offering a different kind of service, he decided to put his ideas into practice with the client.

"I did the usual accounts, but I also benchmarked them, used 'what if' analysis, carried out a detailed trading analysis and also drilled down into what the two directors really wanted," he explains.

When the directors came in for the meeting, he gave them each a piece of paper with KPIs on, including gross profit, net profit, business value and take home pay. Column one displayed the figures for the current year and column two was for them to record what they wanted the figures to be in 5 years' time and he sent them to opposite sides of the room to fill in the blanks. When they both came back with different answers, they really started talking. "That led to us looking at the additional work I'd done and it became apparent from looking at the figures that they had much bigger margins on selling tiles than fitting them. The director who was project manager for the tiling work said, 'I'm not doing that anymore, I'm not going to fit another tile' and sacked himself from that part of the business straight away!"

The original fee from the client was £1700, but after going through all the extra work he'd done, Karl used Time's Up! fixed pricing software to explain the services the client would get if they upgraded to the 4 or 5-star packages. They agreed on the spot to upgrade to 4-star at £4500, with the intention to upgrade to 5-star in the next year at £7500.

Over the next 12 months the client's sales improved by 30% just from the directors focusing on the part of the business that made them money. Even more remarkably, net profit improved by 790%! In fact, at the time of writing, Karl had just checked their performance for the first 4 months of the year and their sales were up 47% again, and they are just about to open an amazing new showroom, which is four times the size of their current showroom.

That first client was so successful that Karl now replicates the process with other clients. "When they see the 'what ifs' it really gets them thinking about the potential in their business," he says. When, as often happens, the business owner says they don't have time to do anything about it, Karl will help to introduce a cloud accountancy package to make the business more efficient, get them to analyse how they spend their time and to really focus on the business. GMR is now actively involved in their clients' businesses, not just preparing their accounts.

This has had a very positive impact on GMR's fees. For new clients average fees are now 150% higher than they would have charged previously. GMR are also offering new services to existing clients, which in some cases has seen fee increases of 160%.

So what has the impact been on debtors? Instead of waiting to be paid in arrears, GMR now uses fixed fees spread across monthly payments. All clients are being converted to Direct Debits; this has had a huge impact on cashflow and debtors.

They manage their clients better so they don't spend so much time on unprofitable work and turnover is up 38% over the two years since they started to make changes. The majority of that increase is net profit.

Karl is now much more confident about the value he can bring to his clients. This has had a positive impact on not only GMR's profit but also the profits and lives of their clients.

The key learning points:

- Have confidence in what you are worth. Look at the value you are giving and what the impact is on the client, not how much time it takes to do the work.
- Step back every so often to look at what you do and see how you could do it better. When you do that, you see the gaps and can spot opportunities. When you give clients more, they often start asking you to do more!
- Work at getting everyone on board and involved with what you're doing. Let the results speak for themselves and people will understand what you're trying to achieve.

A 40% increase in prices in just 18 months – and zero WIP

Established in 2008, Northern Accountants is based in Leeds and has one director and a team of 10.

In this book of extraordinary stories, Phil Ellerby's stands out. When he began his practice he struggled to make any headway, but in just five years he increased the average annual fee his clients paid from £700 to more than £3,200. He moved out of his garden shed to state of the art offices. And from being a one-man band, he built up a team of 10. His focus on pricing has been a key element of this success, bringing him both the profits and the type of clients he wants.

Phil explains what he's done to develop his pricing strategy: "At the start, I chased every single piece of work and ended up with clients who would never have accepted added value fees. Our average fee at the moment is £3,249 and our average intake this year is actually £4,216 for new clients so that's a massive change from the £700 it was at the start."

To be able to charge these higher fees Phil has had to deliver a much higher level of service and he uses the PMI system (*from*

AVN) to deliver business growth services that appeal to more ambitious clients.

This has meant targeting a different type of client. "Our ideal client is all about the actual person. It doesn't matter whether the business is big or small it's what their ambitions are and their attitude towards making a commitment to investing in our services. If they're prepared to invest in our services then we're absolutely prepared to work with them. If they want to screw our prices into the floor, then we don't negotiate on price so obviously we're not the right kind of fit for them."

To attract the right kind of clients, Phil had to look at things from their point of view. "What I had to do was create a service offering that delivered what they needed from an accountant rather than just being a necessary cost. We had to turn ourselves into an asset, something that people buy into and are prepared to pay for in order to get the information that they need to take their businesses forward. If you can create the right service offering you will attract the right people."

The impact of working this way hasn't just been on profits. "If you're working with small clients you might have to do five sets of work in comparison to just one bigger client. So you have to keep five people happy as opposed to one and that's where your work-life balance all goes wrong and you're working 70 hours a week and things are just ridiculous."

Pricing software has been another important part of Phil's pricing jigsaw, enabling him to put up his prices by a staggering 40%. "We have a set pricing structure on the software and we sit down together with the client and it becomes us against the computer! We have a battle to see what we can get the fee down to. I'm always happy with the end result because I set the fees behind the screen and the clients are always happy because in essence they feel that they've picked the right price. Because they can chop and change the services that they want we can strip something out but then put something else in so they find something that's comfortably within their budget. And ultimately if we are still too expensive then we don't win the client.

"We integrate the pricing software with collecting by direct debit and that has probably been one of the best things that we've done. It's enabled our growth and allowed us to take on additional team members because we know when the funding's been coming in.

"It took 18 months to get through the full cycle on the payment structures so that all our clients were on it, but now we know exactly what's going to come in and clients know what they've got to pay and when they've got to pay it."

Clients pay by direct debit over a period of 12 months and that has led to another remarkable result – zero lock up and work in progress. "Our last invoice is on the last day of their financial year so effectively they've paid for everything before we even look at their year end work. So ultimately we have no work in progress, we have no lock up or anything because we've been paid for everything before we even pick up the pens to do the year end."

This integrated approach to pricing, with each element having an impact on the rest, is a shining example of what can be achieved.

The key learning points:

- Move onto fixed pricing and move away from second guessing what clients want to pay based on what they paid before. Create an offering that you have confidence in and that you know delivers value.

- Implement a direct debit collection scheme. It used to cost us £26,000 in financing costs for the credit comptroller, overdrawn bank account charges and so on. On the fees we're collecting this year – which are far more than they were previously – we will have a cost of about £5,000 in collection fees for the direct debit.

CHAPTER EIGHT

STEP 3 —
Educating the client and building the value

This next step in the framework is critical. It is also the one that, as a profession, we are not that great at. You see, it's one thing adding more value, but if the client doesn't understand the value then they are going to see you as too expensive.

Instead we have to make sure that we properly build up the value and communicate it, so that we can educate the client about its worth. For example, I often ask accountants and bookkeepers in seminars and at workshops, *"To what extent do you describe to the client the processes you go through?"* The answer is often, *"Very little"*.

Let's take bookkeeping as a case in point. As a bookkeeper or accountant you might say, *"We will do the bookkeeping for you"*, but do you explain in detail the things that you do as part of that? Do you tell them about all the reconciliations that you do, the checks and the balancing required? The answer I hear is rarely in the affirmative.

Instead we simply assume the client understands what we do – even though the reality is few do. They are not in our industry so we mustn't assume they know what we do. If they don't understand what we do then they won't see the value of what we do. And so they will always see us as being expensive.

Building the value: the two-stage process

The first thing you do is to identify and list everything you currently do. You must do this in as much detail as possible. Do not assume anything about what the clients understanding is.

Let's look at an example; bookkeeping. When you do bookkeeping work here is a list of some of the many things I guess you do:

- Posting all business bank transactions
- Completing the monthly bank reconciliations
- Posting purchase invoices, expenses and cash transactions
- Credit card transactions and reconciliations
- Completing the monthly sales and purchase ledger reconciliations
- Completing the monthly sales tax reconciliation
- Making adjustments for any foreign currency transactions

When you list out absolutely *everything* you do it helps the client understand what you do. It helps them see the value of what you do. And it helps them to see your price as being a fair and reasonable price.

The second step we spoke about in the previous chapter – adding value. What are all the other things you can possibly do to give a better result, and offer a better solution to help the client?

Again, let's take bookkeeping as an example. What more could you possibly do to give a better solution? Here are a few thoughts for you:

- Provide basic management reporting every quarter
- Monitor their key expense codes and flag up when any expense rises significantly
- Maintain their fixed asset register
- Carry out regular adjustments for accruals and prepayments so their monthly profit is more meaningful
- Complete their sales tax returns
- Track and monitor their debtors (accounts receivables)
- Provide regular advice on how to keep their debtors/ accounts receivable to a minimum, collect cash quick and improve cash flow

Use this two-step process to create as big a list as possible and then ensure you communicate every single thing on that list to your clients. Some of the items on the list will form part of your entry-level service. Others you will build into a more expensive package. And some you may choose to offer as optional extras through a subsequent up-sell process.

Your clients don't buy features

Your list is a great starting point. But it is only the starting point.

Everything on the list (everything listed below in the example I have given) is a feature. You may have already heard marketers talk about turning features into benefits. This is because people don't buy features; they buy benefits.

Therefore when you go through that two-step process and create your list of everything you do and everything you can do, you can be pretty sure that everything on that list would be what is called *"a feature"*. For example, if you are doing the bookkeeping work, one of the features might be completing the monthly bank reconciliations.

Whilst you fully understand the amount of time and effort that goes into performing bank reconciliations and the value, do not assume the client does. The phrase, *"Completing your monthly bank reconciliation"* does not convey any benefit.

Features don't sell as well as benefits. Therefore, you need to make sure that you explain the benefit to the client of *everything* you do. In the case of reconciling the bank account you might say something like this to the client:

"Reconciling your bank account on a regular basis is critical. When you get to the year-end, if this doesn't reconcile your accounts will be wrong. You could end up paying too much tax because you've missed allowable expenses. Or you risk fines and penalties from the tax authorities because you've missed taxable income. Or you have to pay higher accountancy fees for the accountant to sort it out.

So what we do is reconcile your bank account every month."

Can you see how much more compelling that is? Can you see how that communicates the benefit to the client who now understands that what you do is much more than just a reconciliation? The client can now see it will help them save money, save tax and help them sleep better at night through less risk of getting into trouble with the tax authorities.

This technique is called turning features into benefits.

The clarity of quantification

Another technique you can use is one I call "quantification". Bookkeepers and accountants are the experts with numbers and so wherever possible we should try to put a number on the value.

Of course, that is not always easy because, as I have said before, value is very subjective. However, in many instances we can put some form of quantification in place. For example, if you are building in some tax planning, you could probably quantify the amount of tax savings.

Similarly, if what you are doing is building in something around helping them to get paid quicker, you could quantify the impact on their bank balance if you can help them to reduce their debtor days or accounts receivable from getting paid on average within 30 days down to 10 days.

When you quantify and put a number on the benefit it creates clarity. It helps make it even more real for your client.

The visual power of the tick list technique

Another great technique you can use is the ***tick list technique***. This is where you list on a piece of paper everything that you do in one column. Across the top of your chart you list your three different packages (remember step 1 of the formula). Perhaps you describe these as your Bronze, Silver and Gold. Underneath each heading you use a series of ticks or crosses to show which of the things that you do are included in or excluded from each of the three different package levels.

This gives a very visual representation of what the client will get within those three packages and communicates your message simply but powerfully. They can see at a glance all the value they get within a package (i.e. all the features where there is a tick). It also helps them see graphically the difference between the 3 packages.

It also shows them what they don't get if they go for the cheaper option.

Once again there's some powerful psychology that takes place here. Behavioural economists have found that as human beings we are loss averse. That means we don't like missing out on things. Therefore, by simply using a visual representation of the things that a client will miss out on if they choose to buy the cheaper option then it will encourage some people to trade up instead to the middle or top option in your list of three-tiered packages.

Beautiful packaging

Of course when it comes to communication the most professional way of communicating all of what you offer and the benefits that such services bring is through a brochure – something I would urge you to create for every service you offer.

There are two reasons for this. Firstly, if you create a professional looking brochure, it is what's known as "packaging" – one of the four 'P's of marketing. By the way "pricing" is also one of the four 'P's of marketing too.

Companies like Apple understand the value of such packaging all too well. This is why the packaging for their products is often described as 'beautiful' or 'exquisite', because what Apple understands is that when you professionally package your solutions it influences the customer's perception of the quality. And when we perceive greater quality because of nice packaging, we ***expect*** to pay a higher price. So I would recommend you package your solutions with a professional looking brochure.

As well as being a hugely useful marketing tool there is actually a second and more important reason for doing this. Your brochure becomes your system and your reminder of what to say. So rather than relying on luck to remember to describe the benefits of all of the things that you do, your brochure does that for you. In the meeting with your client it gives you a structure with which to guide the client through your offer and build up this picture of value.

Real life stories

There are three success stories to close this chapter from three extraordinary accountants who are getting incredible results using this approach. Read what they have to say and the results they are getting.

A structured approach to pricing brings dividends

Established in 2007, Grant Jones is a small accountancy practice in Camberley, Surrey. Fiona Jones is the sole director and has a team of two, bringing in additional sub-contractors when needed.

When Fiona Jones started her practice in 2007 she bought a block of fees to help the practice get up and running. While it was very useful initially she soon realised that one of the characteristics of her client base was that they were quite elderly, with several on the point of retiring. The other key characteristic was price sensitivity. And, while they did make referrals to her, the referrals tended to be of a very similar type.

"So even though they were good referrers there were no real long term business prospects in it. That was my biggest issue," Fiona says. "The challenge has been to break through that barrier. I'm not sure if I've done it yet, but I have started to get bigger clients who are slightly less price sensitive and that's helped a lot. I've had to use a telemarketing company to get my name out there and put me in front of the people that I need to see because there doesn't seem to be any other way of doing that at the moment."

Things began to change when Fiona joined Mark's pricing mentoring group. "It helped to get me in the right frame of mind about how to structure my pricing. Previously it was always a bit hit and miss – 'oh, that's a limited company so I'll charge them a fixed fee of X.' And now that I have two others on the team I'm able to take on bookkeeping work which has helped a lot. If you can get the bookkeeping, generally the accounts and everything else follows."

Pricing software has also made a difference, but what has had the most impact is having a brochure to use in client meetings.

"The brochure explains all the services I offer so it gives me a script which really helps to bolster my confidence when I'm talking to new clients. And as a result of that I've had reasonable success on the telemarketing campaign. I'd say that I've probably more than doubled what I've paid out so far for telemarketing. Obviously the telemarketing campaign was a one off cost whereas the fees I'm getting back in are going to be repeatable every year so that was good."

And the brochure was instrumental in doubling the fee of one new client.

"It was a quote for an estate agent and normally for that size limited company I would have quoted £1200 for statutory accounts and tax returns. But when I went to see the client and ran through the brochure with them and explained everything that was included in the service, in the end I quoted them £1500. They actually came back a week later saying they thought my quote was too light and asking me to re-quote. So that was quite interesting! I then said that I felt that their current accountant was overcharging them so we ended up splitting the difference, which came to £2500, and no bookkeeping. That pretty much doubled what I would normally have charged. I think it was the use of the brochure and the way he was able to go through it and see exactly what I was doing that made the difference."

Fiona now has a much more structured approach to pricing. “We now package our services so it’s clear what you get and what you don’t get. Before, it would be pretty much ‘we’ll do whatever you want’ but now the options are clearly set out for clients and for us. It’s really helped us to streamline what we do and focus on the processes we need to have in place to deliver the service.”

The key learning points:

- Look at the services you’re offering and how much you’re charging for them. Are they profitable?
  Even though I charge a fixed fee we still have time management and time monitoring systems that we complete so I can keep an eye on how much time tasks are taking. I think that’s important otherwise you can very quickly lose track of where you are profitability-wise.

- I’ve never really bothered with brochures before, but they have definitely helped. People seem to like them; it’s something they can touch and look at and go back to as a reminder.

“I wouldn’t have a waiting list of clients if I couldn’t articulate what I have to offer”

Janice Mayer is based in Portland, Oregon and set up her own practice in 2014. Her background is predominantly in industry but she also worked for several years in a traditional accountancy practice before setting out on her own. She has two full time employees and her husband also works part time in the business.

When she set up her own practice the one thing Janice Mayer knew she was going to do was to put fixed billing in place right from the start. She was used to billing for time every three minutes at the very traditional accountancy practice where she’d been working, but she was never happy about it.

“If I was on a conference call with a client or in long drawn out conversations with attorneys, I was usually multi tasking and doing other work in the background. So I never felt it was fair to bill a client for doing the work that I was doing while I was listening to another client that was being billed as well,” she says.

This, along with the problems caused by clients attempting to 'fix things themselves' because they didn't want to be charged for a phone call, made her determined to do things differently in her own practice.

It wasn't always easy; Janice admits that she made some big mistakes at the start and set her prices wrongly when she underestimated how much time a job would take. What put her on the right track was realising that she had to communicate the value she brought to clients.

"For example, I have been working with Intuit since it was a DOS program and have been a pro-advisor for ever. I had created a vast amount of templates, but I wasn't putting value to those templates. And I wasn't putting value to the intellectual ability and capability that I was bringing to the table. Once I could articulate that to the client, they saw the value more as well."

A measure of how well she's ***communicating value*** is that she now converts 80% – 90% of prospective clients – a huge increase from her previous 50% success rate. And she even has a waiting list of people wanting to become her client.

"I have a waiting list of about 12 clients right now and I don't think I'd have that waiting list if I couldn't articulate to them what I have to offer," Janice explains. "I have had clients say, 'I'm going to talk to some other accountants before choosing whom I want to work with.' But I haven't lost anybody because they know what I am going to be charging them upfront and they know they can budget for that. The fact is that what I am doing in my practice is what I am saying that they should do in their own. Obviously I would never tell a client to go out, complete a project and then wait until the end to tell their customer how much it's going to cost. But that's what a traditional accounting firm is doing. They appreciate my way of processing billings because they know what they will be paying for our services."

To avoid the problems caused by clients trying to do things themselves, Janice has also created an innovative way of handling client calls.

"On top of whatever package or processes they choose, I have a fee structure that there is a call fee. So if you want a response within 12 hours, it's going to cost you $500 per month. For that, we will call you within 12 hours and solve an issue with you. And then we go to 24 hours and into 36 hours. That doesn't mean that I am going to wait 36 hours to call that person back, but I will guarantee that within 36 hours I will call you or someone will call you and resolve your issue. And I have not had anyone who hasn't upgraded to either 24 hours or 12 hours. So that in itself is 100% revenue increase because it wasn't there before. And the larger clients who want that 12 hours response have no problem at all coming up with $500 per month."

Paradoxically, one of the things Janice is most proud of is a client who left because she wasn't happy with the fees she was paying.

"She was always unhappy. And she was the biggest pain in the backside you could probably ever work with! Love the person, don't like her work process. When I went through the process of explaining what we were going to do it was actually going to cost her more to continue with our services. And what came out of that is she wasn't a fit for us and we were not a fit for her, but we could separate without her being frustrated and angry. So even though I lost a client it wasn't a loss for me because she then understood what our value is. And it was my fault for not setting expectations right at the start of what we were going to be able to do for her for the pricing."

But, Janice adds, "Will she be back? Yeah, she probably will."

The key learning points:

- Give your clients the power and knowledge to be in control to choose the service they want. Everybody is different. They can be any place from 'All I want you to do is a review' up to 'I want you to do the nuts and bolts and everything else.' If you give clients that power you are going to continue to build long-term relationships.

More clearly explaining services to prospective clients

Martin Woodward of Small Business Services (Accounting) Ltd started his practice in 1996 in Manningtree near Colchester, originally offering management accounting, bookkeeping, payroll and IT training. His son and daughter now also work in the practice, as accountant and bookkeeper respectively, and they have about 25 clients.

For most of the last 20 years Martin Woodward has been happy to let work come in through client referrals, without worrying too much about actively pursuing more. "As long as the money came in, I didn't really think about where the business was going, what it was doing or really anything about the future of the business," he says.

It was only when his daughter came on board five years ago to manage the payroll side of things that he began to see that he actually did have a business. And with his son recently gaining his ACCA qualification and joining the practice too, Martin realised that he needed to grow the business if it was going to provide for all three family members.

His pricing strategy until then had been mainly guesswork. "I'd assess the number of hours of work in my head and go for that, be it right or wrong," he says. "Of course, usually it was wrong and I ended up doing more work for a smaller hourly rate. I'd also look at what other people were charging and undercut that in order to get the work. But I don't think that way anymore."

The difference now is that Martin has started to use brochures that explain his services clearly to prospective clients. And the results have been immediate.

"We had three brochures prepared, for auto enrolment, payroll and bookkeeping. I always knew auto enrolment would be a relatively easy sell for one particular client who appreciates the value that we provide. They know that we may not be the cheapest, but we do give good results and we have a good rapport with them. So I sat down with them and went through an auto enrolment PowerPoint presentation which covers everything that's in the brochure, but in a more visual way. Then, using the Cloud Pricing software, I quoted them the middle option, which meant doing everything in the brochure except setting up the pension fund. I then added that as an optional extra. And they accepted both of those! Just like that they said, 'Yes that's fine. Do it. We know it's going to cost us as a one off, but get the job done. Keep us compliant and get on with it.' The fee we agreed was four times what I would have charged previously. That has to be my greatest success so far with the pricing tool and I'm very very pleased with that one."

It's not just the increased fee that Martin is pleased about. "The client is happy as well. They don't feel ripped off; they feel they are getting good value. And that's what's so nice about this and it obviously demonstrates that it's working."

The payroll brochure also helped Martin to win back a former client who had contacted him about auto enrolment. "I wanted to get back the payroll work as I could see a longer term on-going payroll earning because the client had been doing it herself using the HMRC tools. So although I used the pricing document as a guide I decided that I would offer to do their setup for a reduced fee. It was still more than I would have charged before, but I deliberately kept it low because there was yearly recurring income riding on the payroll. Time will tell if I've done the right thing, but that was my rationale for not sticking absolutely to the pricing document. Nonetheless that pricing document set the benchmark and gave me the comparison. It gave me a figure so I could say to them, 'Look, this normally costs £X, but because you are coming back to me I want to get you on board with the payroll so I'm going to do it for £Y.'"

There have been changes elsewhere too. "We certainly focus now on the type of clients that we want and it's made me think a lot more about not just taking on work at any cost," Martin comments. "One of the things that really puts my back up is when somebody rings up and says, 'How much for a set of accounts?' That now says to me that he's looking for a cheap deal so I don't rush to do that one. But if somebody phones and says, 'Oh, we think you can help us do this, that or the other' then that's obviously a different approach. And we're happy with that because then we can say how we can help and work it through."

Martin has also changed his business cards. "Our old business card said what we did – accounts, bookkeeping, payroll and so on. But we've just had them redesigned to match the new logo and I decided to put something on the back of the business card. Initially I was just going to list what we do, but then I thought, 'No, everybody knows what we do.' So I decided to put a couple of client testimonials on there instead. This is now beginning to work for us.

With a new website in development too, Martin is feeling confident. “We’ve done a lot in the end. It’s taken months and months and months and months and we’ve got more work to do, but it’s really minor. We now have the three wonderful brochures which we can expand upon gradually as we decide the routes that we are taking as a group.”

The key learning points:

- You do have to step back from just being a fee earner – even if it’s only half a day a week – to start looking at what you are doing and how you plan to grow. I’m conscious that we only have about 25 clients, but of course they are 25 clients we do quite a lot of work for. One of the risks with our business model is that if we lose one of those clients we lose a high percentage of our fee income; as much as 20% if we lost the wrong client at the wrong time. Because of the way that I grew my practice initially I really didn’t have a sales pipeline; so you have to ask, where do your replacement clients come from?

- The second thing I would say to anybody is to have that sales pipeline and have that extra work coming in. I know it’s sometimes difficult to cope with extra work, but you must have something to fall back on, some form of potential client. And it takes time. You don’t put a website up and get 20 clients knocking on your door overnight. It can take years to actually nurture clients and get them to trust us and to know that we are what we say we are. Eventually, when the time is right, we know that they will come over.

- Grade your clients. Know your business, know your clients and know the contribution your clients make. Who are the ones that are worthwhile and that earn you money? It's not all about money though. Are they people that you enjoy working with?

- Have confidence in yourself. Learn to think, 'I am worth more. I do a good job.' That's my overall message really and that is my big win, that confidence to go out there and stick to my guns and not waiver. So if somebody says, 'That's a bit much,' look at it the other way and say, 'OK, what can we take out of the service that will help you?' Or, 'I'm sorry, I'm not going to come down any further because I don't believe I can provide the level of service for that money.' It's hard sometimes of course, to turn somebody away, but what we find in all businesses is that you'll get some clients that are high maintenance. You earn very little out of them and they are probably the ones you spend most of the time on.

CHAPTER NINE

STEP 4 — Manage payment expectations

Your payment terms are an integral part of your price. And with some creative thinking can help you get a better price.

But first, why is it that so many accounting firms act as a bank? Why give clients credit?

In 2014 I carried out a survey of 725 UK accounting firms to find out how they priced and how they got paid. In the survey I asked, *"What are your payment terms for compliance work (e.g. annual accounts)?"*

Only 5% said they got paid in full in advance. 21% said most of their fees are payable in advance. The rest – 74% – get paid after the work is done.

Why is that? After all, there is no legal or professional requirement to do so.

Accountants and bookkeepers are in the service industry; and generally the service industry gets paid either in advance or on delivery.

If you go to the dentist for a check up, before you leave, you go to reception, book your next appointment and pay the bill. If you take your car for a servicing, you pay the bill before you get given your keys. And in some services, you would even pay in advance. For example, we generally pay our utility or telephone bills monthly in advance by recurring payment.

Back in 1999 I changed the payment terms in my accounting firm. Up until then I was like everyone else. I got paid when the client felt like paying it... which sometimes was never.

When I changed my system to ask for money before starting the work I did it with trepidation. I assumed everyone would object and I would lose clients. So I gradually introduced it. To my amazement at the time I got so little reaction.

And when you change your payment terms from in arrears to in advance it has a very significant impact on your cash balance.

Clients like to pay up front

The benefits to you of getting paid up front are obvious:

- It improves your cash flow
- You eliminate costs associated with cash collection
- You eliminate bad debt write offs
- Recurring payments create predictable cash flows

And strangely, it benefits clients too.

Firstly, paying up front means there must be complete *certainty* over the price. We've already discussed the importance of certainty.

And if you allow clients to pay monthly by recurring payment then it gives them manageable cash flows. Most people prefer to have a small regular payment than one big one (even if that means paying in advance).

At a more subtle level there are further reasons explained by price psychologists and behavioural economists. They often refer to these as the saliency effect and the timing effect.

Saliency and timing effects

When we take cash out of our pocket to pay for something there is an immediate pain. We feel the loss of that cash. This is saliency.

In contrast, if you go to a casino you swap your hard-earned money for some chips. Armed with your chips you approach the roulette table. Since chips are not cash, as we place our chips (our bets) there is a disassociation with money coming out of our pocket and so we don't feel the pain. It's not real money; merely plastic chips.

This is why many people spend so much on credit card. Because the money is not taken from your bank immediately we don't feel as much pain.

As well as saliency, there is timing. Let me explain it this way.

When you buy a holiday you typically pay for it many months in advance. When you then go on that holiday the payment of it is long forgotten and consequently you enjoy the holiday free from payment pain. And at the end of the holiday you have enjoyed it so much you want to immediately book the next one.

However, if instead you knew you had to pay for that holiday in full on the last day of the holiday (and even worse, you had to pay for it in cash) it would place a cloud over your holiday. You would not enjoy the holiday as much because at the back of your mind you know you have to make sure you still have sufficient cash reserves to pay for it.

Then at the end of the holiday, when you pay for it and experience the payment pain, you are less inclined to go and book the next one.

When we pay for things in advance we are then free to get maximum enjoyment out of what we have already paid for.

A powerful way to tap into these two effects is to let your clients pay you by recurring *payment in advance*.

Many firms I work with set up a recurring payment so they get paid by monthly instalments throughout the year with the final payment timed to coincide when the end of year work is done. Logically it doesn't make sense that clients would accept that. If they've been used to paying for their accounting services 30 to 60 days *after* the service is delivered, why would they agree to start paying up to 365 days *in advance*?

The answer lies in timing and saliency, coupled with certainty and the ability to make small regular payments.

In fact, many things we now buy we pay for by recurring payment. For example, satellite TV. We can now enjoy unlimited movies whenever we want. And we don't feel the pain of payment because that is handled automatically by recurring payment. Whereas if the satellite companies knocked on your door every month and asked you to write a cheque you would be reminded of payment pain every month.

So how do you make the change?

Increasingly accounting and bookkeeping firms are getting paid in advance by recurring payment (in the UK this is using Direct Debit). This is what many firms now do...

If the year end is 30 April they promise their client to have their accounts completed within 3 months of the year end; 30 June in this example. The client pays by monthly Direct Debit over 10 or 12 months (I prefer 12 months because you can use some powerful price psychology).

Those Direct Debits start so that the last payment is made when the accounts are expected to be complete. In this example, 12 months starting July of the previous year.

But how does that work when historically the customer has paid in arrears?

The best time to agree the fee for accounting work is as soon as the previous year is complete. So when you complete the work for the April 2016 accounts have the fee discussion about the work for the 2017 work and then start the Direct Debit so that the client has paid in full by June 2017.

Of course the problem here is they probably need to pay for the 2016 accounts in full (under the old system) – and if they are used to paying 30 days after completion of the work, they will be starting the Direct Debits for the April 2017 account *before* they have even paid for 2016.

This is what the firms I work with do...

Words really matter

The way you describe your payment terms to your customer is important. You should describe it in a way that explains the benefit. This is how many firms I work with describe their payment terms for annual accounts...

> **Our easy payment solution helps your cash flow**
>
> To make your cash flow easy and to help with budgeting our cloud accounting packages are payable monthly in advance by Direct Debit.
>
> And if you have a set of accounts due to be completed within the next year, we even have a range of easy payment options to help with any *catch up*. These include paying by credit card, paying by finance, paying by cheque or spreading the payment across the first few Direct Debit payments.

In practice this is what many accounting firms do...

Let's say the fee for the April 2016 accounts is £1200 and they are completed in June 2016. You are having the conversation with the client in June 2016. And let's say this would normally be paid a month after invoicing, i.e. in full in July 2016.

Let's say you also agree a fee of £1320 for the April 2017 accounts and you would like this to be paid over the 12 months from July 2016 to June 2017 so you are paid in full by the time you expect to complete their 2017 accounts.

First you describe your payment policy (as set out above). You then say, *"To avoid any cash flow issues we will let you pay your*

2016 accounts in 12 interest free instalments of £100 per month. That means you will pay a Direct Debit of £210 per month for 12 months."

Clients do not object to you allowing them to spread the current fee over 12 months by interest-free instalments.

Focus on the benefits

You should re-emphasise the big benefit, *"To make your cash flow easy and to help with budgeting".*

Some firms go further and say, *"The great news is, after 12 months your monthly payments will roughly halve!"* Which is true. Because once they have caught up, their monthly payments will just be for one year (in the example above the £210 per month will drop to something in the region of £110, subject to what the fee is likely to be for the 2018 accounts, which you would discuss in June 2017).

My favourite solution is Direct Debit

In the UK we have a system called Direct Debit. It's a wonderful system that puts both customer and supplier in control.

The supplier is in control because they can extract money from a customer's bank account at any time (provided it has been previously agreed). The customer is in control because they can cancel a Direct Debit any time very easily.

Whilst it used to be very hard (in fact impossible) for smaller businesses to set up Direct Debit, times have changed. My favourite system is GoCardless.

I started to use GoCardless in 2015.

Most of the accounting firms I work with now use GoCardless.

Here are two examples:

"Superb software. The simple act of being able to change a regular Direct Debit, or to charge a one-off amount, is excellent. Payment is pretty quick and fees are minimal. The ability also to have a 'pay link' on your website or in an email is excellent. Once I found GoCardless I never looked back!"

— Jason Blackman, 3 May 2016

"I think it's brilliant. Now a condition for all new clients. And now approaching all the legacy clients to get them on board."

— David Potter, DP Accounting, 3 May 2016

Do you always want to be paid up front?

No. Sometimes you can use creative payment terms to make your price more appealing. This is particularly powerful when you offer different payment plans with your packages. For example, the entry-level is paid in one payment in advance. Your most expensive package might allow the client to spread the payment over 6 months.

The cash flow advantage of the most expensive package makes it more appealing even though the total price is significantly higher.

Your payment terms are a critical part of the pricing process.

CHAPTER TEN

STEP 5 —

Formulate a price that is linked to value

Now that we have built up the value the next step is to come up with a price. More specifically, a price calculated based on the value to the customer. That means we should *not* price based on how long the work is likely to take, because there is no link whatsoever between how many hours you spend doing the work and the value to the customer. Given it doesn't make sense to price by the hour we have to instead price based on value. Unfortunately, as I said earlier, value pricing is hard because value is subjective, and just to make it worse; it differs from person to person.

You will remember earlier I also said that you have to involve the client in the pricing process. You have to have a face-to-face meeting so you understand what they value and what is important to them. But that in itself creates a problem.

When you are in front of a client you have gone through building up the value (perhaps using a brochure) and they are ready to buy from you. They now want to know what the price is. But how do you come up with a price when value pricing is so hard, and not only that, every client's circumstances are completely different?

Take bookkeeping as an example once again. Surely the price will depend upon the complexity; on the size of the client; the number of transactions; the type of accounting system they are using? If it's annual accounts or annual financial statements, the price might depend on things like what trading entity they are, since a limited company has greater requirements than a sole trader, for example.

Payroll meanwhile depends on how frequently the client runs the payroll and how many employees they have. It also might depend on whether they want physical payslips for their employees or digital payslips, and a whole host of other things.

So how do you come up with a price when you are in that meeting with the client and you have been put on the spot? A structure or system is required. Without a system it all relies on luck.

There are some processes we can have for very simple services, so if you are pricing, for example, a simple tax return for an employee and you have created your three options, you might decide just to have a simple fixed price for each of the three different options.

You could also use something called "percentage pricing" where the price is a percentage of the outcome. That can work, for example, with tax planning or with profit improvement advice (although if you are in the US you have to be mindful that generally the IRS does not allow contingency pricing on tax returns).

However, more often than not the service we are offering is much more complicated. We don't know what the outcome is going to be and therefore it's impossible to put a number on the value through quantification alone.

This means that the best way to price – and I believe the only way to properly value price unless you are such a skilled expert you can do all the calculations in your head – is to use a software-based approach. In other words when you are ready to reveal the price you simply open up software, and working with the client and asking them a series of questions to determine what they want, the software comes up with a series of prices for your different options.

The 3 big benefits

There are three big benefits to this approach.

Here is the first one. When you are involving the client in the process and they can see how the price is building up based on their answers to your questions it creates transparency. And with transparency it creates credibility and trust.

There is much more believability when a computer comes up with a calculated price as opposed to you seemingly saying a number that just pops into your head. What happens is because of that greater trust, that greater credibility and believability, people are more likely to accept those prices and are less inclined to negotiate with you.

A second big benefit is that when you use a software-based approach that puts the client in control – since they are deciding how the questions are answered and what features they want – then they spend more money. This stems from the fact the customer is in control. When customers are in control of the buying process, and get to choose what they put in their *basket*, they very often spend more money.

The final benefit – and the most significant – is when you reveal the price only one of two things can happen. Either the price is acceptable and is an amount the client can afford so they say yes and they buy. Or it's more than they were expecting.

Had you sent a proposal through the post or via email then at this point you would have lost control and you would probably never hear from that person again. But because you are in the meeting and the software has come up with the price you are now able to work with the client and involve them in changing the package until it better suits their budget.

You go back and you ask the questions in different ways. You can also offer different options or offer what I call *"behaviour rewards"*. This is a form of discount that you offer in return for the client doing something that makes your life easier.

Through this iterative approach you keep changing the price for as long as necessary until the client eventually says yes. Firms using this kind of approach are getting much higher conversion rates and significantly better prices as a result.

This step is illustrated by seven stories in this chapter – the first of which is a return to Sophia Botchway, who we first met in chapter 5 when she explained how she was getting incredible results moving people onto QuickBooks Online using a system. She is one of my star students and is getting some incredible results within all other areas of her pricing.

Many of these firms are using specific tools and software such as Cloud Pricing or Time's Up! – these will all be explained at the end of this book in the glossary. In the meantime it's time to kick back and be inspired.

Sophia's successes keep coming

Pricing software has also made a big difference to Sophia. Like many accountants, she used to estimate how long a job would take and calculate an annual price based on that. But with software that shows exactly what each level of service includes, clients can see the amount of work involved and are happy to pay a higher price.

She explains, "One of the problems has been that a lot of clients didn't really see the level of work we were doing. They would just see the end result, a copy of their accounts or their quarterly report. Now with the Cloud Pricing software we show them this is what you need, this is what you want for your business, and because they see exactly all the areas we're going to be covering for them when the final calculation comes up, they're not too surprised. In their mind they've already gone through all the stages of the work to be completed and then the price doesn't seem so much."

Using the software has meant that clients have been happy to pay price increases that Sophia wouldn't have dreamt of charging previously. "The second time I used it was a renewal for a client who had been paying us £300 a month. I put the information into the software in front of them, went through the options, and the fee came to £450 a month. And even though it was almost a 50% increase they were happy to accept it."

After the exhausting hours and frustrations she experienced in the early years of Akusika, Sophia has been able to grow her team and take on more clients. “I feel I’m actually running a business now rather than doing a job which is how it felt before. It’s built up my confidence to speak to clients, to speak to my staff and it’s build up the confidence around the office generally because everyone can see the big change within the company.”

A £500 incorporation fee increased to £10,000

Malone Lynchehaun is a three-partner practice with two offices in Northern Ireland, one in Newcastle and one in Newry. They have a team of 11 and offer traditional accountancy services.

Malone Lynchehaun has been in business for 40 years and one of the founders, Sean Malone, still works in the practice. With his two sons now also partners, over the last few years the practice has moved away from the traditional way of doing things and has begun to adopt more innovative solutions.

Brendan Malone explains their approach to pricing: "Timesheets don't tell the client anything about what you have done; they just tell you how long you have spent on a job. They don't tell you anything about the difference you are making to the client, but if you are making a difference that's worth more than just recording the time spent. So we are getting rid of the timesheet except as a way of recording the jobs and to see what everyone is working on at a point in time. We're moving to a fixed price agreement and agreeing the services upfront."

And more than that, the practice is starting to value price too. "Just because it only took me half an hour, if we've done a great job or there's something we are doing extra then you would want to bill that out with the client as well. So if you have done a good job for a client and you saved them a lot of money or really provided good insight into their business, these things are worth more than just the ordinary compliance."

Using value pricing on one client resulted in Brendan's ***biggest fee ever***. The client wanted to incorporate his business and had also been subject to a tax enquiry about six months previously. So Brendan worked in parallel to do the accounts, handle the tax enquiry and incorporate the business. "The tax issue didn't go the way I'd hoped and I didn't get the results that I wanted. So we were a bit disappointed. But then we incorporated the practice and secured the goodwill valuation for £168,000. That will get them a tax saving of about £34,000 over the lifetime with the goodwill." As well as the goodwill, Brendan looked at other areas with potential tax savings and in the end saved the client £100,000 in one year alone.

"I was actually going to send the bill in for £500, just for a basic incorporation and then when I was about to send a quote I said to myself, 'Hold on just a second, you know, that's mad.' I may as well close the business down if we're going to do that. We would never be able to charge for anything ever again.

"So I basically took out the list of what we'd done, ran through the set up and said 'this saved you X, this saved you Y and this saved you Z and there you have it and I want 10% of it.' I said to him, 'I think I've added the value and I've done great work.' And even though the whole thing might have taken a week of work on the timesheet, that might have only been £2000 or something similar. But he saved £100,000 of tax plus another annual amount for the lifetime of the business. So I charged £10,000. It was worth more than just the time it had taken; there was substantial value and I wanted to capture that."

As well as the substantial fee and a very happy client, the experience boosted Brendan's confidence enormously. "Obviously the bigger firms will do their cost questionnaire and other things and sometimes you don't have the confidence that you are doing a good job and you question whether it will make a difference to the client. But when you do something like this and you put in the numbers and well ... the thing is that there aren't too many people doing this type of work."

The key learning points:

- When you are doing something special you need to tell your clients what you are doing and explain that it's not just run of the mill accounts. You have to be able to have that tough conversation with the client to say, "Look, I have done this and it's saved you that. If you were with someone else they wouldn't have done that."

  The clients do respect it once you've spelled it out for them and especially when you can spell it out in pounds and pence. It's very hard to say whether you've improved this profit or you improved that. But when you can say you have saved this amount of tax and the client can see it in his bank account then you can't have any argument about that at all.

Software played a large part in securing a new client

Lockton & Co is based in Grantham, Lincolnshire, and was founded in 1982. The firm is run by Gary Lockton along with his wife and sister.

Unlike many other accountants in this book, Gary Lockton had already been using fixed pricing before he joined Mark's mentoring group.

But he knew that he needed to do more. "We only used fixed pricing for the very straightforward work," he says. "Just tax returns and very basic accounts. What we could never get our heads around was pricing the actual full accounts with the full financial statements, especially for a limited company. I think you'd say we did 'ambush pricing' instead where we presented clients with a bill at the end of the year. Money to me was a dirty word and I didn't like to discuss it or talk to the client about it."

And Gary realised that his 'ambush pricing' policy was actually losing him clients. "I made the same mistake year in, year out. New clients came along that might stay with us for a year, but once they got the bill they wouldn't come back again because they didn't expect it to be as much as it was. So, although we've got 30+ years of experience we were making the same mistakes each and every year. It was really one year's experience 30 times over."

He knew he needed some help to find a better system but struggled to make any headway. It wasn't until he came to one of Mark's seminars and joined the mentoring programme that he began to see how he could change things. And when he later joined AVN and gained access to the Time's Up! fixed pricing software that was the catalyst for a big leap forward.

Using Time's Up! meant that Gary no longer had to talk about money – the software did it for him. As he says, "You are not giving them the price; the software is giving them the price. And because the software is giving the price you are basically divorcing yourself from the process. They have a choice of the 3-star, the 4-star, the 5-star packages and you explain what each one will do in turn and what all the extra benefits are. And you say to them, you choose, how much do you want to pay me to do that work? It gives you the confidence to be able to talk to them and you can still adjust it to suit, but you take out the extras to bring the price into the sort of figure they want to pay. That to me is the crucial part about it."

The software recently played a large part in securing a new client for Gary when a business owner having problems with QuickBooks contacted him. She asked him if he could take a look at the issue and he was happy to help. As he doesn't charge for an initial meeting, he had actually given away his advice for free and he was dubious whether they would come back to him. But a couple of months later he had a call asking him to take over from their accountant.

"She explained the sort of thing she was looking for and at what sort of price. So I took the Time's Up! software and went to meet her. One of the features of Time's Up! is that the price changes according to the standard of the accounting records, so I showed her the accounting systems rating sheet and asked her how she would rate her records. She scored them as average so that's what we put into the software. Well, the price came out at £800 + VAT per month over a 12-month period. She nearly fell off her chair! Even I thought it sounded a lot. I explained that if we could get her accounting records into really good shape, the price would go down and that I could help her do that by moving her onto QuickBooks Online (she was using the desktop version). When we changed the rating to 'very good' instead of 'average' the price dropped to £637 + VAT per month for the 4-star package. She was much more interested then. And when I told her that phone calls and the like were included in that price she couldn't believe it. She said, 'We'll go for that' straight away."

And even better, she was also keen to get Gary's help with moving onto QuickBooks Online. "I explained that there would be a charge for that and how it would work," Gary explains. "We spend half a day or so uploading existing data into the new software and then we do two or three online training sessions. And she was quite happy to pay for everything."

So in the end, as well as the £637 monthly fee for doing the accounts, the client also agreed to pay £89 per month over 12 months for the work on QuickBooks – a total of £8712 for the year.

Understandably Gary is very pleased with the outcome. "Previously, I'd have done what any other accountant would have done without the AVN tools; I'd have looked at what the existing accountants were charging. In fact, they were charging around £3500 and I would have gone in just under that to do the same work. Obviously, we are now using the AVN tools so we can offer the extra added value services, which I wouldn't have known about 12 months ago. I even took along a *BenchMark* report based on their industry just to give the client an overall view of the extra things we could produce. She was amazed. I just wanted to prove the point that we've got a lot of tools at our disposal that probably 90%-95% of other accountants have no idea about." What has also made a big difference – particularly in terms of cashflow – is using the GoCardless payment platform to collect direct debits.

The biggest change for Gary is that he's no longer afraid to talk to clients about pricing. "I realise now that we do accounts; that's all we do and that's all we price for. Anything else should be extra. Now I have no qualms in saying to a client, 'That's beyond our remit of what you are paying for at the moment so there'll be an extra fee and this is what it's going to be. Do you want me to go ahead?' Then I can collect any one-off payments through GoCardless straight away. I would never have dared to say that before, but now I do it and the client doesn't even flinch. And I think, 'What have I lost over the years by not doing this sooner?' and that really, really riles. I get really fed up with the fact that I've lost such a lot of money over the years."

The key learning points:

- Don't be frightened to talk to your clients. I used to think I was doing the work at their pleasure, but my whole world was turned upside down in that respect because now I do the work at my pleasure rather than for them. I do it if it suits me, when it suits me. If they've got deadlines then I'll work to the deadlines, of course. But I like to make sure that I am going to be paid before the work will actually be submitted. So I work for my benefit now.

- Be selective about who you want to help rather than taking in all and sundry. I've started to get rid of some clients that no longer suit the way that I want to work. I get tax returns done quite early in the year now – I had 85% done by the end of June in this last tax season. There were some stragglers so I gave them an ultimatum: pay the normal price if you sort it out within the next 7 days (this was the beginning of December). If you don't get it paid by then, it's going to go up £100 to the end of December and a further £100 for January. One of them didn't even bother to contact me – he did his own return without any further ado. Another client got a bit shirty – she thought I was being unprofessional by saying that to her. I didn't think I was being unprofessional. I still gave her the option to pay the normal price and I told her what the price was going to be. But she moved on and that was actually the result I wanted. I didn't really want that sort of work at that time of the year. So I felt empowered to do that.

From billing a 'fictitious' hourly rate to value pricing

Just Pure is an accountancy practice based in East Sussex, started by Jason Blackman in 2001. He is a sole practitioner with around 120 clients.

When Jason Blackman started his accountancy practice he didn't even think about how he would bill his clients. "Billing by the hour was very much the way to do things in the profession," he says. "So of course, that's what I did too."

But like many other accountants, Jason didn't really know how to price his services and he freely admits that he had an 'almost fictitious' hourly rate.

"It's just so common to hear from practitioners that they don't know what to charge and it's an extremely difficult area. Accountants don't like confrontation with prospects or clients so sometimes it's just easier to go with a low figure and keep the client happy." He found that he was spending a lot of time worrying about how much he was going to charge each client, as he had no consistent pricing structure.

This strategy resulted in a large client base, though with a significant number of them paying unprofitable fees.

It was only when he started talking to thought leaders in the profession like Steve Pipe and Mark Wickersham that he realised there was a better way to do things. "It really hit home that hourly rates are unfair on the client because by nature the bill is always going to be a surprise. I think they're also unfair on us because we're not really charging what we're worth and that's what opened my eyes to the sort of prices I could be charging."

Through AVN, Jason started to use software that gave him a consistent pricing strategy for all clients. "The prices could be rolled out across the board so clients could see on screen what the fee was. They had the ability to change it if they wanted to by taking various services away or adding services on, but they could see there was a structure behind it, not just me plucking a figure out of the air."

With this system now in place, Jason felt confident enough to grade his client list and then take action. "I got rid of all my D clients and that was a massive exercise. I think I ended up with about thirty or forty good quality clients. I decided life was too short to deal with clients that moan all the time about fees and about e-mails you don't reply to within an hour and I now only work with clients that I like – something I believe is massively important."

But he found his real successes came when he put value pricing into practice, particularly for one client who was facing a large tax bill.

"The client was making huge amounts of profits, about £750,000 to £1 million in profit," Jason says. "So they were very concerned about the size of their tax bill. I arranged for a tax expert from AVN to come and see us to discuss various options with the client and eventually the client decided to implement a tax planning scheme. It saved them around £250,000 in tax. So they were absolutely over the moon with that!

"I ended up charging a percentage and earned about £11,000 from it. I was there to hold the client's hand in between all the activity and pass on emails, pass on messages and get the tax expert and the tax planning company together, but I didn't really do any of the hard work. So a fee of £11,000 for what was ultimately two or three days work for me was quite impressive. And the client was very happy to pay me because they saved so much in tax."

Jason has now built his client list back up to around 120 and is able to deliver a high level of service that goes way beyond standard compliance through using cloud accounting systems. "Everything's pretty much automated now and that has helped me achieve a better work life balance because I'm not physically spending as many hours in the office. But in turn it has also helped the clients because I think these sorts of solutions are what the clients need. Real time reporting is the most important thing you can give a client now."

The key learning points:

- Make sure you have a consistent system for pricing, ideally using one of the pricing software packages. When clients can see the price on screen and everything that goes into it, there's far less resistance.
- Put proper systems in place so you don't have to worry about fines and penalties through missed deadlines. If all the basic compliance work is fully systemised, your time is freed up to do the high value work.
- Be happy! "If you're excited about what the day will bring and excited about meeting your clients and working with them, then everyone is happy."

Using pricing software to deliver consistent pricing for the whole team

Richard Brookes started his practice in Cambridge in 2008. He is part of the TaxAssist Accountants network, has around 450 clients and is currently looking for premises for a second office.

Unlike most of the accountants in this book, Richard Brookes started his practice as part of an accountancy franchise (the TaxAssist Accountants network). So rather than plucking figures from the air when he set his fees, he could refer to a fee matrix as a guide to pricing his services. Yet he still felt he wasn't getting it right.

"When I sat with a client I would be thinking, how much will they bear as a fee?" Richard says. "Whilst it might be quite easy when it's a self-assessment, when you're faced with a business rather than an individual it becomes a lot more of a 'black art.' I was always conscious that I was leaving so much on the table, particularly when it comes down to pricing for bookkeeping and other services. You end up trying to guess the number of hours that you might need to spend on something."

What he really needed was consistency in setting his prices, particularly as two other team members were meeting prospects too. Joining Mark's mentoring group and getting the Cloud Pricing software seemed to offer the solution he was looking for.

"I wouldn't necessarily pretend that in every meeting with a prospect we've had the computer switched on and used the software. But we certainly do for incorporated businesses, particularly if they want things like bookkeeping and VAT returns."

And the very first time he used the software he saw the benefit. The client was a start up café and once all the figures had been entered, the mid price fee that came up was £377 per month.

"I saw that," says Richard, "and I inwardly sat back and waited for some kind of objection. But it didn't come. The questioning was much more around the different levels of service. The cheapest package was never an option because they looked down the list and said we want that, we want that, what does this mean, what does that mean, can we do this, can we do that? And it wasn't even a sell; it was just explaining what some of the things meant, what some of the differences were. They asked me to put it in writing, which I did, then we signed the T&Cs and off we went. It was a very smooth process. Previously I would have charged around £150 per month."

And Richard is particularly pleased since the business is a start up. "Start up businesses can be quite labour intensive. So it's working very well for us to be able to give them as much handholding and advice as they really need. We would have done it anyway, but over time that would have meant drifting further away from the amount that was being actually billed. And that would have then prompted another conversation at some point down the line, probably reasonably soon after setting the initial fee. It's quite uncomfortable to have to bring up pricing again. So this will serve us well until we come to a year into the relationship when we're due to have a fee review as part of the natural process."

Knowing that pricing is going to be consistent no matter who is running the prospect meeting has taken much of the strain off Richard.

"I'm more relaxed and more confident in what's going on. So I can now go off to look for premises for our second office. It's a big part of the overall objective of enabling me to step back from that part of the process and not be 100% reliant on me holding the client meetings."

The key learning points:

- The obvious one is to use pricing software; it really is an investment that pays dividends. If it had been available when I started – even though I had a fairly good growth curve – the average fee per client would have grown substantially a lot quicker. It enables you to meet your objectives that much quicker and even to work three days a week. It leads to a lot fewer objections come the time when you deliver the price. And of course the really key thing is when you sit there and you say, 'OK, if the price that's coming up doesn't work for you, let's have a look. Are all the things that are included in the package really necessary for you at this point in time?' You can take things out to reduce the price rather than just cut off 25% or some other arbitrary figure.

Price consistently and not based upon how you feel on the day

Starfish Accounting is a two partner practice with a team of three part-time employees based in Maidenhead, Berkshire. The practice started up in 2011 and has approximately 200 clients with GRF of around £130,000.

When Georgi Rollings set up her accountancy practice in 2011, her previous experience was in large corporate firms; in fact, she had never worked in a small practice before. So when it came to setting her prices, she was in the dark about how much to charge. "I had a look around the internet to see what other accountants were charging and then copied that, which wasn't the best strategy," she says now.

The strategy did get her started though and with regular price increases over the last four years Georgi felt that her newer clients were being charged a reasonable rate.

"But we hadn't reviewed what we were charging older clients. So we still had people on much lower fees because they came on at an earlier stage. And we really didn't have a good grasp of how to charge for more expensive work, like incorporation projects or multiple jobs for our bigger clients. There were lots of things where we just weren't charging at all – we were functioning as a charity! We have always had clients who are poor payers and we don't treat them consistently. So some clients have different arrangements from others and some of them definitely take advantage."

Two things have made a big difference to Georgi: Direct Debits and pricing software.

"We're putting every new client onto Direct Debits now. It's great because there's no argument about it, we just say, 'Oh, we do Direct Debits; here's the piece of paper.' It means we've got a lovely chunk of money coming in, in the middle of the month, without having to go to any effort to chase it. So that's really helped."

And pricing software has proved equally successful.

"We've started to use the Time's Up! pricing software (from AVN) which is great for pricing consistently. We know we're treating everybody the same way and there won't be a day when we're feeling a bit 'weak and weedy' so we charge less or we're scared of asking for too much and we wimp out! So we're much more consistent with everybody who comes in the door. And we're finding it much easier to sell more work using the software too. On average the clients that are coming in the door now are paying 20% higher fees than before and they're also signing up for more services."

One client, for example, is now paying fees of over £4,500 instead of the £3,000 he was paying previously. "There are some extra services in there like a VAT health check, but I wouldn't have charged for that before. This time, I worked though some of the detail and found that things were in a much worse mess than he realised. So I went back to him with a very clear list of what needed doing and I used an extra work order to show him the different areas where he needed more support, exactly how much we wanted to charge for it and what the time scales should be. He signed up to another £3,250 of fees paid over 3 months. I had to have another meeting with him to make sure he was confident that the work was needed and he said, "Yes, that's brilliant. I am confident in you. You go ahead and do it." I feel that we go about things in a much better way now."

Georgi has now begun the process of reviewing the existing client base and charging for work that she had historically done for free, for example, filing accounts for a dormant limited company. And her experience has been that clients are happy to pay for the work when given a price.

One case in particular has given her the confidence that she's now on track with her pricing. "My partner previously worked with a client at a different practice. They had been charging £1500 and as that practice has been around for a long time, I assumed that they'd be better at pricing than we are. The client had concerns about a few issues so we sat down and went through Time's Up! with her to try to address them. As we went through all the possible services, thinking that she wouldn't want them, she'd say, 'Actually I do want that.' We added in more and more services and we ended up with almost £5,000 of fees, compared to the original £1500. Previously we might have felt reluctant to ask for more when the client was already paying us a decent fee, but that's not a good way to run a business."

And Georgi has noticed another benefit too, in the type of client the firm now attracts.

"We are definitely taking on clients who wouldn't have signed up with us before. Just talking through the list of our services means that we are able to demonstrate that we approach things in a different way from other accountants. I recently signed up a client who is interested in extra tax planning and other things that I would never have thought to talk about before. He had met any number of accountants before, didn't like any of them and before we even talked about money he said, 'I am going with you.' So we are able to sign up more interesting clients as a result. It's quite a major mind shift and the way we're going about things now feels much more like we are running a proper business, on a really solid footing."

The key learning points:

- First, make sure you have the ability to do consistent pricing where it's not dependent upon how you feel on the day. It could be a spreadsheet with some sort of menu based pricing where you put people into the correct slot, but preferably use a decent pricing tool. That consistency makes sure you don't do anything stupid.
- Second, use something like Direct Debits to make sure you get paid. It's a real struggle when you sign up clients who agree to pay you and don't. Having the certainty that you will be paid gives you more flexibility to take on more staff, for example.
- Third is having that ability to talk through all your different services. Previously, if we didn't think it was relevant we wouldn't talk to clients about what else we could do. But you really miss a trick when you do that; you aren't necessarily giving people what they need and you aren't giving them the best service.

Give clear and unambiguous prices

Patrick Cracroft-Brennan is a Chartered Accountant and sole practitioner from Oxford in the UK.

Patrick is on the Court of Assistants for a small City livery company, which has only three employees, two of whom are already over 65. They had not yet decided how to handle the issue of auto enrolment and the Clerk was looking at quotes for setting up a compliant scheme with NEST.

When, at one of the Court meetings, Patrick voiced his view that NEST wasn't the best option, the Court asked him to compare NEST with the NOW pension, The People's Pension and any others he wanted to investigate. Patrick agreed to do this and also included the AVN Simplicity Pension in the comparison. He used the Cloud Pricing software to come up with a guideline price for the administration work leading up to the company's staging date and also gave every member of the Court a copy of the auto enrolment brochure (personalised with his firm's details).

Patrick's prices were significantly lower than the quotes the Clerk had already received, but nonetheless he was very surprised when the Court awarded the work to him – particularly as he hadn't even asked to be considered!

“Two things stood out for me,” Patrick says. “Being able to give clear unambiguous costs thanks to the Cloud Pricing software; and the booklet, which everyone said they found very useful. A lot of the online literature around auto enrolment is written from the IFA’s or the pension provider’s point of view. The booklet sets out the practicalities of auto enrolment and very clearly states what the accountant will do for his or her client.”

CHAPTER ELEVEN

STEP 6 —

Make your price seem smaller than it really is

Let's just quickly recap where we have got to in this 7-step formula.

In step 1 we are creating different options using menu pricing.

In step 2 we are adding more value.

In step 3 we are communicating the value.

In step 4 we are explaining payment terms;

In step 5 we are calculating a price that is linked to value.

Now with step 6, having come up with the price, we want to make that price appear as small and insignificant as possible. This is where we start to use the power of price psychology.

This is one of my favourite areas of pricing because it is so powerful.

There is a branch of psychology called *psychophysics*. It has been around for over 100 years and concerns the study of how our senses and perceptions relate to different physical stimuli. What we learn from this field of study is something profound about price.

One of the things that has been discovered is we are completely clueless about price. Instead research has shown that our judgements of monetary value have much in common with sensory judgements. In other words we are acutely sensitive to differences but not so sensitive to absolute values. We might know which colour of two shades of grey, for example, is the darker and which is the lighter, but we don't know the absolute colour.

It's the same with weight. For example we might know, if we have two boxes, which one is the heavier but we will be unlikely to accurately tell the exact weight of each item.

It has been found in this branch of psychology that it is exactly the same with our perception of price too. We haven't got a clue about the price of anything, and actually, when we think about it, it makes logical sense. Price is just an arbitrary number; there is no science behind the price. Unlike weight, colour, temperature, there isn't a scientific scale to give an exact number. We can measure how much things weigh with precision. We can measure colour using a scale like CMYK. We can measure temperature. We cannot measure price; it is just an arbitrary number.

Because we don't know the price of anything, whenever a price is revealed, we have to look at other things to compare it against to give us an idea of whether it seems like the right price or not. That is what always happens when price is revealed, we look to see what price other things are, and so the great thing is we can influence that process taking place in the minds of our customer. That is the world of price psychology.

The stupidity of hourly rates

Consider hourly rates. Bookkeepers will typically charge £20-£30 (perhaps $45 in the US) per hour. If you quote an hourly rate to a client of, let's say, £30 per hour the customer has no idea whether that is the right number or the wrong number; it's just a number.

Because of that they will make comparisons in their head with something else. Now of course there are many things they could compare against; they could compare that against the cost of one of the country's leading barristers who charges out at £600 per hour, and they could say, *"Wow, £30 per hour, now that seems very fair and reasonable"*.

But they won't. What they are more likely to do is think about Janet who they employ as a secretary in the office and pay £10 per hour. Now by comparison your £30 per hour seems expensive. It's three times the price. That's outrageous!

That is the problem with an hourly rate. Whatever number you come up with it will always seem expensive to the client because it doesn't convey any value. Instead it will seem expensive compared with something else they choose to think about.

You need to get control of the process

Instead you need to come up with some other ways of helping the client to see the price as being reasonable, rather than outrageously expensive (which it almost certainly isn't). And that is where price psychology comes in.

I am going to share with you in this chapter two extremely powerful techniques that you can use. Techniques you can use to show your price in the best light.

Don't reveal the headline price

The first of those is what I call, *"don't reveal the headline price"*. What do I mean by that? Well a headline price is the total price. Let's imagine for a moment that you are pricing, for example, moving someone onto a cloud accounting system. Let's say that you decide that you have a single fixed price of £495.

Now if you have been paying attention you will already know that is not a pricing strategy I would recommend. You need to give people options as we have talked about and not offer your services too cheaply.

But nevertheless, let's imagine that we have set the price at £495. A better way of expressing that to the client would be:

Five easy payments of £99

The final total is the same but by breaking it into smaller chunks it has a profound impact on the client's perception. People perceive that five payments of £99 seem smaller than £495 even though the math says they are equal.

This has been proven through extensive research. For example, back in March 1998 in the Journal of Consumer Research, John T. Gourville published an article called "Pennies-a-day: The effect of temporal reframing on transaction evaluation". He noticed that to increase transaction compliance, i.e. whether somebody buys, marketers sometimes temporarily reframe the cost of a product from an aggregate one-time expense to a series of small on-going expenses, often in spite of the fact that the physical payments remain aggregated. This is shown to significantly influence subsequent transaction evaluation and compliance

Of course, you may think this won't work because surely people know what's going on. They do the calculations in their head and realise they are exactly the same. Curiously that is not the case.

It's not the case because, as demonstrated in the world of behavioural economics, we are very lazy when it comes to decision making. We take shortcuts. Most people can't be bothered to do the math. In the case of the example above they focus on the £99 and not the £495.

In fact this was demonstrated in October 2005 by Mazumdar, Raj and Sinha in their research paper, "Reference price research: Review and propositions" published in the Journal of Marketing. In this paper they explained that whilst people know that comparing a monthly price with a total price it doesn't matter. People usually compare reference prices subconsciously.

Now we see this working in other industries very successfully too. The leasing industry is a classic example. If you want to lease a car for three years, the flash ad showcasing the brand new fancy Mercedes car will say, *"You can have this car for just £399 per month"*.

What they don't tell you is the headline price – the total amount you would pay over that three year period because it may cause you to think again. Instead they give you a monthly price because it seems more affordable. It seems a lower price.

There was some research done recently by one of the US' leading Internet marketers Ryan Deiss. He tested payment options by selling online digital products for $197. At that price 340 people purchased, generating revenue of $66,980.

He tested offering the same product but this time for two payments of $97 (almost the same headline price, i.e. $194, which is close to the $197). The impact was phenomenal with conversions increasing significantly by almost threefold to 977 people purchasing and generating revenue of $189,538.

That was fascinating and a strong enough result in itself. But it gets even more interesting.

Deiss decided to test further to see what would happen if, instead of two payments of $97, it were three payments of $97. Now if you do the math you will realise that's actually a 50% increase in the price. And you would expect a big reduction in conversions (sales) when the price is increased by 50%.

And yet the increased price had little impact on conversions which once again went up, this time to 1,008 purchases making the total revenue $293,328, or nearly five times the revenue generated the first time he offered it at a total headline price of $197.

What happens is people focus on the $97 and not the $291 (which is the headline price in the third test, i.e. 3 lots of $97).

So the key take-away here is that you always want to reduce the price to as small a number wherever possible. That means with your recurring bookkeeping work and your recurring annual financial statements you should quote the price as a monthly figure, not the annual figure because clients will see the monthly figure as being a smaller overall price than if you show the headline figure.

The price-order effect

When you present your prices, does it matter how they are presented and in which order?

Actually, it does.

Another powerful area of price psychology worth considering is the 'Price Order Effect'. Back in 2012 Suk, Lee and Lichtenstein carried out some research and their research paper, "The Influence of Price Presentation Order on Consumer Choice" was published in the Journal of Market Research. Let me describe to you one of the experiments they carried out.

Taking a bar price list, which listed the beers from the cheapest beer at the top through to the most expensive beer at the bottom, they measured beer sales over a period of time. After doing that they adjusted the menu, swapping the order to list the most expensive beer at the top and the cheapest at the bottom and again measuring the impact on sales.

They found that the average spend was significantly higher when the beers were listed from the most expensive through to the cheapest. This is because when we look at a vertical list of prices we tend to read from top to bottom, and so the first price we see, the first price we read, and therefore the most expensive beer in the second case, creates a frame of reference by which other prices are evaluated and judged.

So if we start off with the cheapest one first, and that is the first one that we read, then we see everything else as being more expensive; and therefore we are more likely to settle on buying a cheaper beer. If on the other hand we start off by revealing the most expensive first, then everything else seems much greater value in comparison and we end up settling on a higher value purchase.

There is another aspect here as well and that is the concept of loss aversion something which behavioural economists have found that we suffer from. I also mentioned this earlier when I discussed the *tick list technique*. We associate price and quality as being related. When we see the prices going down, as we read down the menu, we associate that with a loss of quality. So we recognise that as we go down the list we are giving something up, which in the case of the beer price experiment influenced consumers to go for a higher priced beer, because they become reluctant to sacrifice quality.

Now in that particular experiment they were looking at beer prices on a vertical scale. If you are presenting your three different options you might present those on a horizontal scale. If you are to do that, then the price order effect still comes into play, only this time when things are on a horizontal scale we usually read from left to right.

So you want to make sure that if you use the tick list technique and you reveal the price of your three different options, the expensive one should be on the left and your cheapest option on the right, because people will look at the left one first and that will create the reference price by which they judge the other two.

Price psychology is a fascinating subject and I teach 25 different techniques that we can use in pricing. Perhaps at some point I will have the opportunity to teach you some of the other strategies out there but for now stick with these two because they are so powerful.

CHAPTER TWELVE

STEP 7 — The power of testing

Once you have carried out these first 6 steps in this formula, the client should already be buying from you and at a higher price.

Step 7 in the formula is what I normally call the 'Power Strategies', and in this chapter I want to focus on one of them. I refer to it as the Power of Testing. Simply put it means that you need to be continually testing your price because there is simply no such thing as ***the right price***.

I often find accountants and bookkeepers saying to me they are not ready yet to reveal their pricing because they are not sure they have got it right. Well here's the thing, you will never get it right. That is because price is subjective; it differs between every single person and so you will never know what the right price is. The important thing though is there's always a better price, and what you need to do is find that better price through continually testing.

Without a system or benchmark, testing is very difficult. If you always produce a price in your head there is little basis for testing. But when you have a system in place you can systematically test. For example, in step 1 we looked at the power of menu pricing, and so when you create your three different options you can then start to test.

Let's say you have a tax return preparation service and you have three choices and you find, for example, that most people are buying your cheapest level offering. That is telling you perhaps there is not enough value in the middle and the top options to persuade your clients to buy. Or it may be telling you that the jump in price from the cheapest to the middle price is too great. So test something, change it, make it a smaller jump or add more value and then test again and see what proportion of people buy the different options. I can guarantee you will see a difference.

Now of course with testing you should only change one thing at once. What is fascinating about menu pricing is that you know you have got your price about right when about 60% of people buy the middle option, and what you should find is that of the rest more people buy the most expensive option than the cheapest option. So if you are finding 15% of people are buying the cheapest option, 60% buying the middle option, and 25% buying the most expensive, you have probably got it about optimal.

I refer to this as the 25:60:15 rule.

If everybody is buying the most expensive option that is telling you that you are too cheap and you perhaps need to change your packages or add in a super-premium approach.

That is what I love about menu pricing. Once you have got your three-tier structure it gives you a benchmark by which you can then test and measure; and then make changes, and see if the overall results improve.

In step 5 of the formula I talked about having a systematic approach for value pricing, and the software approach. Again, when you have a system like that you have got a benchmark to test against. This is because you are pricing in a consistent way using a precise calculation, rather than simply making a number up that comes into your head. Then you can make a change; you could try putting the price up by 5% and see what happens. If you get no resistance then you know that you have got a better price, and you keep testing and testing and finding that better price. That's the power of testing.

And that concludes the 7-step formula.

In the next chapter I am going to look at something that is a strange phenomenon within the profession, and that is *"why do we keep giving stuff away for free?"*

CHAPTER THIRTEEN

Why do we keep giving stuff away for free?

From time to time I carry out benchmarking studies of the accounting profession, and in those studies I ask how much firms charge for various services.

What is fascinating is that I find there are a significant proportion of services that are commonly given away for free. We have looked at one already; setting people up on a cloud accounting system where typically 30-50% of people are doing that free of charge.

Other services in the UK for corporates include an annual return and sometimes we might also act as a registered office. These are both also often done for free.

For example, in 2014 I published my Research Report, "How much do your competitors charge: And how your accountancy practice can price much more profitably." I surveyed 725 accounting firms in the UK and asked how they price for certain accounting, tax and bookkeeping services. When I asked how much firms charge for preparing an Annual Return for a limited company, only 39% said they charged a separate fee. For acting as a Registered Office for a corporate client it was only 32%. And for completing the paperwork for a dividend amazingly only 18% charged a separate price.

That's incredible.

Most firms either didn't offer the service, openly admitted they do it for free or they bundle it into their fees (which amounts to doing it for free).

The list goes on...

Another thing we forget to charge for is the mortgage reference letter, which is completed by an accountant for self-employed business people looking to get a mortgage. Again in studies that I have carried out, between 40% and 45% of accountants carry out this work for free, despite its value to the client.

Why do we do all this stuff for free?

The implications of doing this are huge. We might not think of it as being big because each of these services very often are relatively small things, but small things soon add up and for many firms it could be tens of thousands of pounds worth of potential fees that we are giving away completely free.

So why are we doing this?

Well, the reason I think is often because we feel we should. We justify it by saying "It's a good quality client, they pay me a good fee for their annual statements and for their benchmarking, and though they have just asked me to do something else, something new, I'll do it for free because I don't want to upset them."

But that's wrong.

I think the real reason is we don't know *how* to price it, and it is more effort to try and figure out how to price it, and then have a price conversation with the client, than to simply just get on with it and do it. That is not a great reason.

We should always be mindful that if we are doing something that has value to the customer – and value includes taking away hassle and saving the client time – then we should price for that.

Of course the great news is you now have a structure. You have a 7-step formula that you can use to price any service.

An inspiring story

So I am going to leave you in this chapter with a final story to illustrate this. It is a story I came across recently by an accountant I have known for many years called Bob Hurn.

He had the opportunity to price something that was a new requirement imposed on businesses in the UK. It was only a small amount of work and was the sort of thing that typically an accounting firm would do for free but Bob saw the value in it and was brave enough to price it accordingly.

I shared Bob's story with the firms that I mentor and many of them took action, copying what Bob did and reporting back to me. In all cases they made a significant amount of money and extra profit that in the past they would have just given away for free without thinking about. So read Bob's story and think about all the things that you currently do that you don't charge for. And think about how now charging for them could positively influence your bottom line.

The total impact of pricing a service normally given away free

Bob Hurn is the owner of Hurn accountants in Reading.

Bob has started to charge for small jobs that he would previously have done for free. When new legislation came in requiring most companies to have a register of Persons of Significant Control (PSC), he calculated that it would take about 10 minutes to do the work for each client and decided to charge a fee for doing it.

"We emailed all relevant clients," Bob says, "And advised that we should be charging £75 + VAT, but as theirs was relatively simple (most have one or two PSCs) we would prepare the register for £35 + VAT, subject to being instructed by 29 February 2016. This allowed us to do the work at a time that's traditionally quiet for us." They also advised clients of the information they needed to record if they wanted to prepare their own register.

Within 24 hours 20 clients had instructed them, the work had been done and £700 invoiced!

To date more than 50% of their clients have gone ahead with the work and Bob estimates it will generate at least £3000 of fees.

"We may have left money on the table as the take up has been so rapid," he adds, "But we are feeling very content as we would just have 'thrown in' simple jobs like this in the past. Two clients have decided to prepare their own register and it feels nice that we gave them the option rather than imposing another fee on them."

Changes to the Companies House annual return have also brought new opportunities. Bob previously passed on the £13 fee to his clients, but charged nothing for his time. As the new Confirmation Statement that replaces the annual return is a completely new document, he will be making a charge for the service and estimates that this will bring in revenue of around £5000.

CHAPTER FOURTEEN

What about clients that can't afford you?

So you have gone through this process and you have clients that still say you are too expensive or they can't afford you. Well, that will always be the case. The thing is you cannot act for everybody; you should only act for the right clients.

Instead you need to think about who is your ideal client. What are the sorts of people that you want to work with? And if they can't afford you then they are not the right type of client. However, I want to tell you a story in this chapter of a particular type of client that you probably come across, and that's business start-ups.

When I started my accounting firm back in May 1996, I was a start-up myself. Over the next two years for some reason I seemed to attract business start-ups, and because in those days I thought it was all about building up as big a client base as possible I would always take them on.

I would then find that they had lots of questions, such as what they needed to do to set up their books and records; who they had to tell that they were now running their own business and what did they have to tell the tax authorities? Ironically those small start-up clients therefore often required more help in the early phases, more hand holding, more support, and more questions answered, than my clients that were established businesses.

And yet I didn't know how to charge them because there wasn't anything that needed doing. There were no accounts needed until they got to the end of their first year, there was no tax return needed doing, and I wasn't doing the bookkeeping work.

So I would continue to help them, answer their questions, set their bookkeeping up and set them up with the tax authorities. Back in those days I did keep timesheets and I made a note of the time I'd spent on their questions and handholding.

Then, a year or so later when they reached their first year end and the first set of accounts and tax returns needed doing, I would contact them again. But there would sometimes be a nasty surprise waiting as I found that in some cases those clients hadn't made it through the first year. Whilst they had gone out of business I had built up time on my ledgers for which I would now never be paid.

Even for those that had survived the first year in business there were some that couldn't afford my accounting fees and so they went somewhere else or did it themselves and again I never got paid.

Only a small number of business start-ups I worked with did end up paying me and even in those cases I never recovered the time spent in the early phases helping them get up and running.

So a few years later I came across this concept of the ideal client profile, and I thought to myself that perhaps business start-ups were not the type of client I should be taking on. Typically, many of them don't have much money and they require much more handholding and support than an established business.

But is that enough reason to turn them away?

Business start-ups can turn into great clients, so to have a blanket policy of not taking on start-ups might not necessarily be the right approach.

It was at this point I had started to understand value pricing and I decided that what I would do is to create a business start-up package to suit the needs of this audience.

I asked myself what do start-ups need and came up with various options. They need help with some bookkeeping training, they need setting up with the tax authorities, they perhaps need some financial advice, they might need pointing in the right direction for getting finance with the bank. It seemed obvious that these sorts of things I could bundle into a package, and then I could have another level where I could build in some training. I could also add value within a premium package by including help and support on running a successful business. I could build in a mentoring programme at the most expensive level.

Also at the top level I could let them be part of a 'business club'; I could do some business consulting sessions, help them with their margins, their pricing, their marketing, their cash flow.

So I created these three different packages and I assigned a price to each of them. These prices were reasonably high at the top level, a couple of hundred pounds per month, and I decided that if I was to take on a business start-up client that they could only work with me if they bought one of these three packages.

Just to be clear, these packages did not include the end of year financial statements or tax returns; that was a separate price to be discussed separately. This was simply a service that they had to buy where I would do everything I could to help them maximise their chances of being successful and getting through that tricky first year, helping them with getting their books up and running; giving them some business advice and so on.

So what was the result?

When I introduced this service offering what I found was some business start-ups couldn't afford it; they weren't willing to invest a few hundred pounds per month, and so my view was that if they weren't willing to invest in a good quality accountant to make their business successful then they weren't sufficiently serious enough about their business and therefore they weren't right for me.

Some clients though bought one of the three packages and when that happened that gave me the budget to be able to do more to help them be successful and get them through that first year.

Inspiring stories

I taught that system to accountants I work with and I want to share with you two stories now of firms that have created something similar and the results they are getting.

The first of those is a sole practitioner called Lance Thomas. The second one is an incredible story from Stewart Newberry. He is actually two stories in one. He talks about his pricing of the business start-up service but also another service that, very often, accounting firms in the UK give away completely free. He put in place a system and the numbers are incredible.

So enjoy those two success stories.

A lesson in how to deter price-fixated clients

Lance Thomas of LCT Accounting is a sole practitioner based in Cheltenham whose practice has been operating since 2013. He is the sole employee but outsources work to a range of contacts and suppliers.

As a start-up business himself, Lance was keen to help other new businesses looking for an accountant. "Having worked in industry for many years I went through the pain of trying to set myself up in business with limited funding and being very careful about what I was spending. So I understand what it's like to take that step and how difficult it can be."

Lance found that – just like him – the businesses that were approaching him wanted the cheapest option. "Initially I'd think that maybe I could help them and I'd start to do things for them," Lance says. "But the pain point was that I was working for, what I now see in hindsight, were ridiculously small fees because I needed the work in the early stages of my practice. Also, they needed a lot of support and over time it became more of a domino effect. So we'd start off doing the work for a particular agreed fee, but then other things would begin to creep in – 'Can you just help with this?' or 'I just need help with that.' And whilst I was building up relationships with the clients, I'd often end up doing a lot of stuff free of charge or at very low rates. So, yes I was building up good relationships, but I wasn't earning anything!"

It became obvious to Lance that he couldn't continue in the same way. He was offering a flat fee to cover all the work he did for start-ups, but he realised that while some clients wanted help with everything, others only used a part of what he offered. He decided to try out tiered levels of service.

"I introduced grade scales, so I had a 3, 4 and 5-star service. The 3-star service was very much the package that I used to offer, but even with that I was able to price it differently to how I did originally. I raised the price by about 10 or 20%."

Lance's 4-star service added on more support that would be really valuable to start-ups, such as help to set up their accounting and bookkeeping systems and accounting software, as well as a meeting with a consultant.

At 5-star level the support became even more valuable when he brought in experts such as IT consultants and graphic designers who could really help a new business get off the ground fast.

"The new packages were priced well over what I priced before. As a result of this, I found that many people were slightly reticent about the fees, but they did at least understand the service I was offering. Often they would go away and think about it and, whilst some would still go back to the much cheaper options they can get elsewhere, I found that more and more were coming back to me and really appreciated the value of the service."

One of the key selling points was that Lance would tailor his service to the specific needs of the client. While some start-ups needed a lot of help with the accounting side of their business, others were already comfortable with that but needed, for example, to have a logo designed for the business. "So I was able to introduce them to graphic designers and we came to an arrangement whereby I would include that in my start-up package," Lance says. "I would bill the client and the graphic designer would bill me and I found this has been a much easier way to get through to people. New clients saw me as a one stop shop for their business and I have continued in that way".

One of Lance's clients came to him when he had just set up in business as a plumber and had no accounting structure or any experience of handling his accounts. Lance's service was more expensive than the other accountants the client was considering so Lance took time to explain exactly how he could help him.

"I recommended an accounting software package and some consulting to help him get set up, so he could report his numbers accurately. He was very good at plumbing but he wasn't great at doing the bookwork! I explained that he could invoice this way, record his numbers that way and so on, to make it a really smooth process. And the longer the conversation went on, the more he was able to understand and appreciate what that meant. It didn't get him anymore interested in accounts, but at least it made sure he understood what to do. Then when he looked at my fees, although he could see I was a bit more expensive he could also see what he was going to get and what that could save him in the longer term."

The client's business is now thriving and Lance attributes that in part to the clarity of the financial information. "Because he has very clear and precise financial reporting he can make good decisions for the business."

Lance now finds that most new clients opt for the 4-star package, which is priced at four times the fee for his minimum package. And he's also found that his way of working deters potential clients who are simply looking for a cheap deal. "Clients who are looking for low fees are not clients I want anymore and I am able to pick this up quickly in conversations so I can politely move them on. In fact, some clients who I took on early with low fees now realise that I tend to price differently and I'm also losing those as well. It's disappointing from a personal point of view, but from a business point of view it's good!"

The key learning points:

- Understand the value of what you do and learn how to explain the value to your clients so they can see how it relates to them.
- Be enthusiastic about the owner's business. If they believe you're as interested in it as they are, they will want to work with you.

"Clients aren't price sensitive, they're value sensitive"

Stewart Newberry is a sole practitioner running his firm, Positive Practice, from two offices on the Yorkshire/Lancashire border. He has a team of four and is a general practitioner dealing with small business clients.

Stewart Newberry has been in practice for nearly 13 years and for almost all that time he has used price to gain a competitive advantage. "There are an awful lot of small practices around and there's always been competition on price. We'd get an excuse to look at the accounts for a prospect and see how much their accountant was charging. If we couldn't match it, we tried to explain why we were slightly higher, but if it was a fee that we could clearly match we'd probably undercut it," he explains. "It wasn't a very effective way of pricing."

For one particular service – acting as a registered office – Stewart charged a maximum of £100 per year, but often made no charge at all. And when it came to helping to set up a new business, he would offer a free meeting to the business owner and give them a lot of valuable advice, in the hope that they would come back as a paying client. "We gave away all of our knowledge. All of the things that they should be valuing as prospects and clients we gave away for free," he says now. It was only when he joined Mark Wickersham's mentoring group that he started to see that he could do things differently.

"We looked at the real value that the registered office service could provide to a client and we created three service packages around a registered office offering. The cheapest starts at £39 a month and the most expensive five star service is £80 per month. We selected 20 clients to test it out on and of those we actually got five to buy into the new service straight away. Four of them went for the cheapest option but even then we were instantly making far more money just on those four than we ever did before.

"And then we had one client who really was keen that he got the best service. He signed up for our five star service so he's paying us £80 a month plus VAT. To be honest, we're not actually doing any more than we did for the last four years for his dormant company when we were charging him £100. But we're getting almost nine times the price we got previously."

Stewart is certain that the reason it was so successful was because he didn't focus on the price. "We focused on the value to the client, so our proposition was what we could deliver to them. We explained what we did, day in day out for all of our clients in a more detailed way, why we did certain things and what value that gave them. That's what sold it – so I didn't have to".

And another key factor was looking at the service packages from a non-accountant's point of view. Before they were finalised, Stewart's administrator went through the wording to make sure it was meaningful for the client, not just for an accountant. "The focus was 'what does the customer want?' and 'how will this help them in their situation?' It was very customer focused as opposed to technically focused or even service focused. That's how we really earned this. Most accountants don't normally do that, sorry to say."

Perhaps even more remarkably, Stewart didn't even need to have a sales discussion with his clients to sell the new service. "We included the new service packages in our annual renewals," he says. "It consisted of three sheets of paper with a table outlining the different service packages, with ticks and crosses in nice bright green and red just to make it stand out. Two pages were actual detailed descriptions of what each of the service elements meant to the client. Then there was a sheet saying 'yes, please deliver this service to us' and they signed it and sent it back. We then sent them an email to complete the direct debit."

Stewart then applied the same process to start-up businesses. Instead of offering an initial consultation where he gave away all his valuable advice for free, he devised the PositiveStart programme. New business owners can now buy a pack for £195 which gives them guidelines on getting started in the right way, simple forms for HMRC like 64-8 and CWF1, books to help with record keeping and a copy of Michael Gerber's E-Myth, the best-selling guide for entrepreneurs.

But again, there's also a range of support packages to go along with it.

"The support packages run for 10 months and go from £39 to £149 per month depending on which level they choose," he says. "The majority we've sold so far have been our three star package where the initial £195 is paid and then they sign up to £49 per month. For that they get an hour's phone conversation each month plus ten helpful resources over the ten month period. We cover everything from getting your books right for your accountant through to how to sell on the internet. The higher level packages also include free cloud computing software and help to set up and use it."

What's more, the relationships Stewart is building up over the course of the support packages mean that the business owners are more likely to turn to him for their accounts work when the time comes.

Stewart estimates that this service alone will bring in around £10,000 per year – for something that previously made no money at all.

The key learning points:

- Think of the value that the client receives, not the costs to you as an accountant. Something may seem very simple to you, but if it's something the client really values you need to recognise that and price it according to the value.

An update on the story since Stewart was originally interviewed in 2015

Since January 2016 we have now introduced the 3/4/5 Star service package system to all our new and existing clients (based on the principle of our PositiveStart services as described in the article). We took the opportunity to re-engage our client base using the "customer focused" services and at the same time increased our annual fees to 90% of our client base, bringing in an extra 18% increase in profits (on our current client base).

The customer focused approach to services packages has also helped us convert more of our prospects and for higher fees, such that if the trend we've seen over the past months continues for the whole year we could see our turnover increase by 50% year on year.

Many thanks Mark, you set us straight and we're following through on the foundations you help set.

CHAPTER FIFTEEN

A truly inspiring story

Do you remember Jane Aylwin's story right at the start of the book. Back in February 2016 she provided an update on the story. She posted the update in a Closed Facebook group consisting of US accountants and bookkeepers who are part of my mentoring programme.

Whilst I have tidied up the formatting of the post and some of the grammar, it is what Jane wrote. This is what she said...

"

Where do I start?

In Thursdays' meeting the question was asked by a few... WHERE DO I START?

Great question, and I spent far too long wondering about that when I started working with Mark Wickersham in April last year –

all the same concerns that I am sure you have – how will I keep my clients, how will I know whether I'm charging the right price, what if I'm too expensive, what if I'm still too cheap.

The very best advice I can give you is to JFDI (just flippin' do it). Sure, you will make mistakes but how many times are you getting it right, now?

I know I got it wrong more times than I got it right and I had nothing to measure what I was doing and why it was right or wrong – now I have all the information I need to make sure that I keep getting better at this and keep getting better results.

My sorry tale

But, if you have a bit more time to read this, here is the longer, slightly sorry tale, of how I actually did it.

I've been working for myself for 12 years and started to actively build a business in 2013, so for 11½ years I was making the *same mistakes over and over*. When it was just me, it didn't really matter; I earned a good hourly rate and that was all I needed really – or so I thought.

When I started to build up my business it became more and more apparent that charging by the hour was really not working. Apparently, no-one else can do the same amount of work in an hour that I can and I was finding it hard to justify charging all those hours on to clients.

Then there were the hours that staff weren't doing client work. What was I supposed to do with them? Basically, I was working harder and harder and harder and more and more hours, just to pay my staff.

That was becoming... annoying.

I was scared to change things

So I went to see Mark speak at a conference and joined the mentoring program.

I soon understood what an amazing difference the things he was teaching me would make to my business... but I still didn't do it because ***I was scared to change things***.

Then I heard someone say, *"If you do what you have always done, you will get what you have always got."* Kind of obvious really I guess, but that was what it took.

So I committed to making the new systems work for me – I sat with the software and I ran virtually all of my existing clients through it and I tweaked it and I played with it until every single time, the price came out at least 50% higher than I was currently charging for the essential level, at least 75% higher for the full level and more than 100% higher for the premium level.

And then I started to price new prospects using the software and the brochures (well, the copy for the brochures printed in the office anyway) – I didn't get the first couple, but I didn't have time to do them anyway, the prices were still too low and it was great practise. I then tweaked the software a bit more and tried again – I had a couple of successful sales meetings with new prospects, converted them to clients and gained confidence in using the software, understanding the prices and talking about the value of what we do.

An extraordinary journey

Then at the beginning of November I had a meeting arranged with a client – a nightmare client whose paperwork is a complete mess, who wasn't paying us nearly enough but who I have been working with for four years and who I happen to quite like on a personal level – I am sure you all have some of those?

On my way to the meeting – at 6.00pm in the evening (as that was the only time they could do) I asked myself just what on earth I was doing… I worked my butt off all day and then went to an evening meeting with them because it was convenient, *for them*! I was worried about asking for more money – why did I feel I needed to keep them anyway?

So I decided as I walked in through the door that I was going to put my fee up. I talked them through the 'new' service packages I was now offering, ran them through the pricing software, and walked out the door with ***a 175% increase in fees***, a happy client, a better relationship and much less grouchy than I had been on my way there.

And then I did the same thing with the next three meetings that week – I added nearly 12% to my turnover in that week, with four existing clients, for really no more work.

I'm no longer just paying the staff

Since then, I have secured a further 24% of my original turnover figure, with JUST three new clients, doing what I love and building some fabulous relationships in really short spaces of time. Because I'm happier, because I understand what I'm offering, because I believe in what I'm offering AND because I'm getting paid the right amount to do it.

I'm still working really, really hard, but there's a much better reason for doing the hours – it's to grow my business, not just to pay the staff!

So back to the original question – *where do you start?*

Grading and analyzing your clients

Start with analyzing your existing client base and getting the prices right for them in the software – and remember – the prices should always come out higher than what you are currently charging. You know in your heart what you would really like to earn from these clients and performing this exercise will help you understand what you should take into consideration when setting up the software.

- What is it about that particular client that means you need more from them than from another one?
- What is it about each industry that means they need a higher or lower price?
- What additional questions do you need to add to identify what the price should be?
- How can you separate out your services to build value and cross – and up-sell, rather than including everything you do as standard?

Then set up the software to reflect what you are learning. And don't be afraid to keep tweaking it as you learn more.

Once you have done this look more closely at your client base; you've just had a long hard look at what they are paying, so now's a really good time to do it. Grade them and decide whether you really want to keep the 'D' list (we *'Ditched the D's'* in our practice – it was liberating). Is there anyone on there you don't mind losing? I bet there are some that you can definitely do without!

Explain to them that you have changed the service that you are offering and you would like to talk through it with them – don't increase your fees, ***change your service***. Give them the opportunity to decide whether it's right for them and if it's not, part company.

There were some I just ditched – it was really hard to do, but it is SO nice not to have to work with them anymore – I have no idea why we do it to ourselves!

Also try it out on prospects you don't really want or need – great practise and if the price comes out wrong, you can always choose not to take on the client.

Then move on to clients that you want to keep but are not paying enough – again, don't increase the price; change the service and take the time to explain the value in the new service packages you are offering.

I wish I'd started this years ago

It is all time consuming but you don't have to do it all at once and you leave with either less unprofitable work and more time, or higher fees for the work you are already doing.

Once you gain confidence with it talk to the clients you want to keep and meet the prospects you want to convert.

I found that, having taken six months to actually get started, it was no time at all before I found it really easy and I was really comfortable having the conversations. I ***just wish I'd started this years ago***; I would be in a very different place right now if I had.

Consistency is the key

I use the system in every sales conversation I have now and *it works*.

When I'm asked to price a service I haven't already got a resource for I no longer shout out the first figure that enters my head in a moment of panic. I go away and I write a resource giving three service options and explaining the value in each separate element. Then I talk the client or prospect through it.

To me this demonstrates consistency. And consistency is key, It shows the prospect that I have a system and this really helps them have confidence in the price."

GLOSSARY

Within the stories in this book the accountant or bookkeeper occasionally makes reference to products that may not be familiar with you. Here is a quick glossary of these terms.

AVN
AVN is the UKs leading association of accountants. Steve Pipe FCA founded it in 1998, and I became a co-owner and director in 2003. All over the UK, hundreds of accountants are using AVN resources, tools and support to help them become more successful, more profitable and enjoy what they do much, much more. You can find out more here, **www.avn.co.uk**

BenchMark
This is an AVN software tool enabling UK accountants to benchmark their results against other UK accounting firms and also, more importantly, for benchmarking their clients.

Cloud Pricing
This software tool makes it easier for you to sell more accounting, bookkeeping and tax services to more clients at better prices. I created it in 2015 to provide accounting professionals with a systematic approach to value pricing; an approach that embodies all of the strategies, techniques and price psychology I teach. You can find out more here, **www.pricinginthecloud.com**

GoCardless
This is a very popular software application for enabling businesses to set up recurring payments. At the time of writing it is the leading Direct Debit solution in the UK.

PMI
This is an AVN product, which stands for "Performance Measurement and Improvement system." It is a packaged solution that takes accountants core product, annual accounts, and makes it much more valuable.

QuickBooks Online (QBO)
QBO is one of the leading cloud accounting tools currently available. Intuit (the company that owns QBO) is currently the biggest accounting software company in the world, and as you'd expect from the market-leading company, the pace of development and innovation is extraordinary. It's my favourite cloud accounting tool and the one I use in my business.

Receipt Bank
This is one of many tools helping automate bookkeeping data processing. It is frequently mentioned in the stories because it is an extraordinary solution used by most accounting firms I work with. You can find out more here, **www.receipt-bank.com**

Time's Up!
This is an AVN pricing software tool designed to be used live in front of clients to produce a fixed price agreement. I originally created this software tool within my own accounting firm back in 1999 and it's been used by thousands of UK accountants over the last 16 years as part of AVN's solutions.

BIBLIOGRAPHY

This is a list of some great books on pricing, behavioural economics and other related topics that are important in the pricing process.

Alan Weiss, *Value-Based Fees*

David W. Cottle, *Bill What You're Worth*

Dan Ariely, *Predictably Irrational*

Hugh Williams, *Life Without Timesheets*

Leigh Caldwell, *The Psychology of Price*

Michael V. Marn, Eric V. Roegner, Craig C. Zawada, *The Price Advantage*

Peter Hill, *Pricing For Profit*

Rafi Mohammed, *The Art of Pricing*

Reed K Holden and Mark R Burton, *Pricing with Confidence*

Robert B. Cialdini, *Influence: Science and Practice*

Robert J. Dolan and Hermann Simon, *Power Pricing*

Ronald J. Baker, *The Professional's Guide to Value Pricing*

Ronald J. Baker, *Pricing on Purpose*

Ronald J. Baker, *Implementing Value Pricing*

Steve Pipe, *The UK's Best Accountancy Practices*

Steve Pipe, *The World's Most Inspiring Accountants*

Steve Pipe and Elisabeth Wilson, *Stress Proof Your Business and Your Life*

Steve Pipe and Mark Wickersham, *Your Blueprint for a Better Tax Practice*. The Tax Club

Steve Pipe, *The Good, The Bad and The Ugly*. Accountancy Magazine July 2008

Thomas T. Nagle and John E. Hogan, *The Strategy and Tactics of Pricing*

Thomas J. Winninger, *Full Price*

Tony Cram, *Smarter Pricing*

William Poundstone, *Priceless*

Mark Wickersham, *Effective Pricing for Accountants*

Mark Wickersham, *How Much Your Competitors Charge*, 2014

Mark Wickersham, *How to Build a Successful Bookkeeping Business*

Mark Wickersham and Steve Pipe, *How to Build a Better Business*

ABOUT THE AUTHOR

Mark Wickersham – *Chartered Accountant, public speaker and #1 best-selling author* – is known as the most sought after **profit improvement expert** in the accounting community. He is famous for helping accounting firms **double their profits** in less than 18 months without having to work harder or do any uncomfortable marketing.

Mark is passionate about this great accounting profession. He believes that we have the power to make a profound difference to the lives of our clients and in return **accountants should be very richly rewarded**. Unfortunately the reality is very different; benchmarking studies show over half of accounting firms are actually making a true economic loss.

Mark wants to CHANGE that.

He is passionate about the accounting profession and helping accountants to become much more profitable. He believes every firm – including you – has the potential to double profits using the **7-step "Fastest Way To Double Your Profits" formula**.

He also strongly believes that the old business model (the way accountants are taught to run accounting firms) is not only commercially stupid, but UNETHICAL. We owe it to our clients to change our focus. This is something Mark learned the hard way.

Don't make the same BIG mistake Mark made

Mark started his own accounting firm in 1996 and made dozens of stupid mistakes in the first 2 years. Mistakes which had disastrous consequences on his profits and cash balances. But in November 1999 all that changed. With help from Steve Pipe, Michael Gerber, Paul Dunn and Ron Baker he created the **7-step "Fastest Way To Double Your Profits" formula**.

Not only did this completely transform the profits of his own accounting firm (which enabled him to sell it in a management buy-out a few years later), it has helped 100s of UK Accounting firms. For example...

Phil Bessant (a sole practitioner in Newport) recently wrote, *"Wow! I've added over £100,000 to my fees (which will all be extra profit) in just a few short months by following the step-by-step advice and systems in Mark's Effective Pricing for Accountants programme. And it was so easy to do."*

And Phil Ellerby (a sole practitioner in Leeds) wrote, *"Mark's simple step-by-step guide... has increased my GRF by 400% in just 2 years, earning me over £220k."*

This 7-step formula is transforming accounting firms.

Number 1 bestselling author

Mark is also a widely published author on practice issues. In May 2011 his book, *"Effective Pricing for Accountants"*, was a number 1 Amazon bestseller. He has also co-authored "Your Blueprint for a Better Tax Practice" and "Your Blueprint for a Better Accountancy Practice", both of which have been widely acclaimed.

Mark has over 100 recommendations from accountants on LinkedIn; CONNECT with him on LinkedIn to get access to free resources Mark has created for accountants in practice.